THE WES

Ellen Raskin

AUTHORED by

COVER DESIGN by Table XI Partners LLC
COVER PHOTO by Olivia Verma and © 2005 GradeSaver, LLC

BOOK DESIGN by Table XI Partners LLC

Published by GradeSaver LLC, www.gradesaver.com

First published in the United States of America by GradeSaver LLC. 2017

ISBN 978-1-60259-893-5

Printed in the United States of America

For other products and additional information please visit http://www.gradesaver.com

Table of Contents

Biography of Ellen Raskin (1928–1984)

"I try to say one thing with my work: A book is a wonderful place to be. A book is a package, a gift package, a surprise package -- and within the wrappings is a whole new world and beyond."

Ellen Raskin was born in Milwaukee, Wisconsin in 1926 and grew up during the Great Depression. Raskin entered the University of Wisconsin-Madison at the age of 17 with the intention of majoring in journalism. During the following summer, she visited the Chicago Art Institute and saw the first major exhibition of non-objective art. She changed her major to fine art and received a disciplined education in the fundamentals of anatomy, perspective, light and shade, color, and techniques of painting and sculpture. Raskin married Dennis Flanagan in 1960, had a daughter, Susan, and moved to New York City. She later divorced, and took a job in a commercial art studio where she learned to prepare other people's artwork for the printer.

During this time, she learned to do paste-ups and color separations at work. While on her own, she experimented with typography using a bench printing press and ten fonts of type she had purchased. She developed a sample book containing ephemera she designed and printed using woodcuts and, after two years, she began a freelance career as a commercial artist. Raskin illustrated for *The Saturday Evening Post*, pharmaceutical house journals, and book publishers. During these years, she made illustrations of all kinds, including more than 1000 book jackets (including the original jacket for the 1963 Newbery winner, *A Wrinkle in Time,* by Madeleine L'Engle) and more than a dozen other children's books.

After fifteen years of illustrating the ideas of others, Ellen Raskin had an idea for a picture book of her own, *Nothing Ever Happens on My Block*, published by Atheneum in 1966 with Jean Karl as editor. Gradually Raskin found that she could turn down commercial assignments and concentrate all her time on her own children's books, each one an exercise in problem-solving for her and, often, for the reader as well. Almost all of them, picture books and novels alike, develop some aspect of the theme that things are not what they first appear to be. Raskin's delight in wordplay is evident throughout her books. Although she considered herself an artist first and foremost, she was awarded for her writing: *Figgs & Phantoms* (Dutton, 1974) was named a Newbery Honor Book and *The Westing Game* won the 1979 Newbery Medal for distinguished writing. Both books were edited by Ann Durell at E.P. Dutton, as were all of Raskin's novels. In all of her work, Raskin made a singular contribution as a humorist. Her highly original, zany -- but always ordered -- humor marked much of her writing, illustration, and book design. She once indicated that her attitude toward humor was influenced by the Preston Sturges film, *Sullivan's Travels*.

When she was asked to name the people and experiences that most affected her work, she listed "Blake, Conrad, Hawthorne, James, Nabokov, Piero della Francesca, Calude Lorrain, Gaugin, Matisse, *Fantasia*, Oriental art, baseball, hockey, zoos, medicine, and Spain," in a *Top of the News* interview published in June 1972. Her spouse Dennis Flanagan reported on Raskin's success as a "finance capitalist" in his biographical essay published in *The Horn Book* in August 1979, to accompany her Newbery Award acceptance speech. Until her death in 1984, Raskin lived with her husband, daughter, and son-in-law in a two-family house in Greenwich Village; this house provided the setting for *The Tattooed Potato, and Other Clues* (Dutton, 1975). It was there that Raskin maintained her studio, her personal collection of first editions, and her stock portfolio.

Regardless of the forces and people that shaped Ellen Raskin's work, one can say unequivocally that her creative process was always guided by her respect for children and her appreciation of fine bookmaking. The books she wrote, designed, and illustrated have continued to take young readers to a whole new world... and beyond.

The Westing Game Study Guide

Originally, Ellen Raskin, the author of *The Westing Game*, entered college at the University of Wisconsin-Madison with the intention of majoring in journalism; however, after visiting the Chicago Art Institute and viewing an exhibition of non-objective art, Raskin opted to change her major to fine art. After graduating with a fine art degree, Raskin moved to New York City where she became a commercial artist. Raskin was a commercial artist for fifteen years before she published her own picture book, *Nothing Ever Happens on My Block,* in 1966; she later decided to write primarily children's books, which culminated in her publishing *Figgs and Phantoms* in 1974 (later named a Newberry Honor Book).

In 1978, Raskin published her magnum opus, *The Westing Game,* a mystery novel that involves 16 supposedly unrelated heirs of Sam Westing, a rich, but reclusive businessmen who dies suddenly, leaving his heirs with the opportunity to win 200 million dollars—if they can discover who killed him. The novel, which is an homage to the mystery novels of Agatha Christie, showcases the different viewpoints of the 16 heirs as they try to discover who murdered Samuel Westing.

Shortly after the publication of the novel, *The Westing Game* won the Newberry Medal for distinguished writing in 1979. For a number of reasons, *The Westing Game* is a compelling novel that captures young readers with characteristics that are not present in typical children's literature. *The Westing Game,* like many murder-mystery novels, features numerous red herrings and plot twists that create a memorable experience for the reader. Furthermore, even though the 16 heirs face off against each other to attempt to win 200 million dollars, Raskin subverts the characteristic endings of murder-mysteries as the characters in the novel eventually benefit from their involvement in the competition. The novel even features elements of adult murder-mysteries such as compelling, well-developed characters, witty language, and unreliable narrators. Thematically, *The Westing Game* also discusses themes such as greed, the negatives of arranged marriages, and revenge.

The Westing Game still has a prominent place in popular culture nearly 50 years after its publication. In 1997, *The Westing Game* was adapted into a film version titled *Get a Clue.* Furthermore, in 2012, *The Westing Game* was ranked ninth among all-time children's novels in a survey published by the *School Library Journal.* The novel remains popular in classrooms across the world, as it is widely taught in English classrooms in grades 4-9.

The Westing Game Summary

The Westing Game is a murder-mystery novel set in Wisconsin during the 1970s. A mysterious realtor arranges for a specific group of people to become tenants in an apartment building called Sunset Towers that overlooks the abandoned mansion of Samuel Westing. A diverse group of unconnected people, both families and individuals, live together in at the Sunset Towers until a young girl, Turtle, discovers the body of Sam Westing after entering the Westing mansion on a dare. After his body is discovered, the tenants learn that each of them is considered heirs to the Westing fortune and are invited to the mansion to hear the will. Sam Westing's will claims that one of them is the murderer and divides them up into pairs and gives them each clues to solve the mystery of who killed him. The winner will receive 200 million dollars. At first, the pairs do not work well together, but eventually each of them brings out the best in each other and the Sunset Towers tenants begin to work together to create a community and solve the mystery, even in the face of adversity when a mysterious bomber begins to terrorize the apartment building. Eventually, Turtle discovers the truth: Sam Westing is alive and is using the game to vindicate himself from the mistakes of his past by ensuring that each of the heirs can have a better life than they originally had. Turtle ends up discovering that Sam Westing has been disgusting himself as various members of the community, each with one of the four directions in his name: North, South, East, and West.

The Westing Game Characters

Turtle Wexler

A smart young girl with a talent for the stock market, she has a long braid and kicks people in the shins. She solves the Westing game.

Angela Wexler

Turtle's beautiful older sister, she's engaged to Denton Deere. However, she is unhappy that most decisions are made for her.

Grace Windsor Wexler

She is Turtle and Angela's overbearing mother. An amateur decorator, she spends most of her time preening over her daughter Angela's upcoming nuptials.

Jake Wexler

He is the husband of Grace Wexler, a podiatrist, and a bookie.

Doug Hoo

He is a high school track star and son of Mr. and Mrs. Hoo.

Mr. Hoo

He is the owner of Hoo's restaurant on the top floor of Sunset Towers. He is generally cranky and very competitive. He sued Sam Westing for stealing his invention of the paper diaper.

Madame Hoo

Mr. Hoo's second wife from China, she speaks very little English and only desires to return home, even if it means stealing.

Flora Baumbach

A single dressmaker, she becomes a mother figure to her partner Turtle and it is revealed she lost her daughter years ago.

Sydelle Pulaski

She is a receptionist who fakes an injury to get attention by walking with painted crutches. She gets very close with her partner Angela.

Chris Theodorakis

He is a wheelchair-bound boy with a nerve disorder that makes it difficult for him to speak. He is brother to Theo and an expert birdwatcher.

Theo Theodorakis

He is Chris' older brother who wants to be a writer but never went to college. He mostly takes care of Chris.

Judge J.J. Ford

She is a local judge and the daughter of one of Sam Westing's servants. Sam Westing paid for her schooling and now she is determined to win the Westing game.

Sandy McSouthers

The doorman of Sunset Towers, he has a drinking problem and may not be who he says he is.

Berthe Erica Crow

An older devout cleaning woman, she spends her life devoted to religious penance for some previous sin.

Otis Amber

The local delivery boy, he brings tidbits of gossip to the apartment complex.

Denton Deere

A medical intern and fiancee of Angela Wexler, he helps Chris get the medicine he needs.

Barney Northrup

He is the realtor for Sunset Towers.

Julian Eastman

He is the current owner of Westing Paper Products.

Ed Plum

He is Sam Westing's lawyer.

The Westing Game Glossary

Senseless

Without meaning or purpose

Demeaning

Something that a person does that causes others to look down on them; an action that lowers a person's dignity

Eccentric

Unusual and over-the-top

Thy

Archaic for "your"

Refine

To make something perfect

Heirs

People in line to an inheritance

Shorthand

A style of handwriting that uses symbols to abbreviate words

Alibi

Proof that a suspect in a crime was in a different location at the time of the crime, and therefore not guilty

Bookie

Someone who takes bets on sporting events

Bribe

To illegally give someone money so they will do what you want

Dastardly

Wicked and cruel

Nosegays

Small, sweet-scented flowers

Procession

An organized body of people walking in a formal or ceremonial manner

Relentless

Harsh or inflexible

Abstention

When a participant in a vote does not vote

Paraphernalia

Equipment, apparatus, or furnishing used in or necessary for a particular activity

Wasting

Gradually reducing the fullness and strength of the body

Traumatic

Psychologically painful

Vengeance

Punishment inflicted or retribution exacted for an injury or wrong

Ragtag

Untidy, disorganized, or incongruously varied in character

The Westing Game Themes

Lies and Deception

The most evident theme in *The Westing Game* is the theme of lies and deception, and the power of lies and deception. From the opening chapter of the novel, Ellen Raskin, the author, utilizes deception to mislead and trick the readers as she introduces a character named Barney Northup, who according to Raskin is not a real person. However, this is only the beginning of the lies that frequent the novel. As the novel progresses, many of the characters in the novel - such as Sandy McSouthers, James Shin Hoo, Sydelle Pulaski, and Turtle Wexler - use deception to obtain their true desires or hide their identity. For instance, Sydelle Pulaski fakes a debilitating leg injury in the opening chapters of the novel, and she hobbles around on crutches for the remainder of the book. In this aspect, she uses deception to receive attention as well as make people feel pity for her. Alternatively, Sandy McSouthers, one of the four identities of Samuel Westing, constantly deceives the other Westing heirs with incredibly sly lies and deception, distracting characters such as J.J. Ford and preventing them from discovering his true identity. Moreover, many of the characters such as James Shin Hoo and Jake Wexler often lie about their professions, as they do not want their counterparts to discover their past (and current) job histories.

Greed

Another prominent theme in *The Westing Game* is the theme of greed. In Chapter 7, the 16 Westing heirs are informed that they are participating in "The Westing Game," which is a game crafted Samuel Westing. The heirs are broken into pairs, and they are then told that in order to win the game, they must discover who killed Sam Westing. According to Westing's will, whichever pair discovers who killed Sam Westing will win 200 million dollars. After the pairs discover that there is a prize for winning the Westing Game, nearly all of the characters become extremely greedy and suspicious of everyone around them. Not only do many of the characters refuse to share their clues, but throughout the novel, many of the characters attempt to undercut other Westing heirs by lying to them, stealing their clues, and distracting them. Although it makes logical sense why the heirs would become greedy and selfish, the actions of some of these characters threaten the lives and reputations of other characters as they attempt to win the prize.

The Pitfalls of Arranged Marriages

In *The Westing Game*, one of the underlying, but rarely discussed themes, is the commentary on arranged marriages. Early in the novel, it is revealed that Samuel Westing's daughter, Violet Westing, drowned on the eve of her wedding. It becomes clear that Violet actually committed suicide due to the fact that she did not want to get married. In Chapter 15, J.J. Ford discovers that Violet loved George Theodorakis, the father of Chris and Theo, two of the Westing heirs. However, Violet's mother was forcing Violet to marry a man she did not love, a senator who served a jail term for bribery. Rather than marry someone she did not love, Violet decided to commit suicide to avoid the arranged marriage.

Later in the novel, it becomes apparent that Angela Wexler is involved in a relationship that almost feels like an arranged marriage. Angela's fiancé, Denton Deere, is a successful intern, who seems destined to have a stellar career as a doctor. While Angela's mother, Grace, eagerly encourages Angela to marry Denton for his future wealth and social status, it is clear to the reader that Angela does not desire to marry Denton. Angela often leaves when Denton enters the room, and it is common for her to barely say more than two to three sentences to her future husband. Angela obviously feels societal pressure from her mother (and other members of the Westing Game) to marry Denton, but one can assume that Angela does not want to marry Denton whatsoever. Even though Angela's engagement is not arranged by her parents, it certainly feels like an arranged marriage; Angela seems to have no choice in finding her significant other, as society has decided that a pretty, young woman such as herself must marry a man like Denton Deere, who will certainly climb social ladders in the future.

Both of the aforementioned relationships act as arranged marriages, and they showcase how Raskin may perceive arranged marriages from her perspective. There are no positives to be gained from either of these two relationships displayed in the novel.

Revenge

One theme present in *The Westing Game* is the theme of revenge. However, this theme only truly applies to two characters in the novel: Samuel Westing and his ex-wife, Bertha Erica Crow. Halfway through the novel, it is revealed that Violet Westing, Sam's daughter, committed suicide after she learned that she could not marry her sweetheart, George Theodorakis, but instead had to marry a crooked politician. After Violet's death, Sam Westing's wife became an alcoholic, and she later divorced Sam before seemingly disappearing. Later in the novel, though, the reader discovers that Samuel Westing had no issue with Violet marrying George, but his wife was the one who attempted to force Violet to marry the crooked senator.

At the beginning of the novel, Sam Westing states that the point of the Westing Game is to find the person who murdered him. Although the characters take it as a literal murder, Sam is actually referring to the person that murdered him emotionally: his ex-wife. Near the end of the novel, Turtle Wexler and J.J. Ford begin to realize that Samuel Westing is making the characters participate in the Westing Game, so he can bring emotional distress to his ex-wife, who is actually Bertha Erica Crow in disguise. Moreover, at the end of the game, Bertha Erica Crow is revealed to be the "winner" of the Westing Game, as she is the one who truly killed Samuel Westing with her decision to force Violet into marriage. In fact, the whole point of the Westing Game is to make Bertha Erica Crow feel the shame, pain, and embarrassment that Samuel Westing felt when his daughter committed suicide. Even though it seems minuscule in comparison to his daughter's suicide, Sam obtains his revenge with Bertha Erica Crow's suffering throughout the Westing Game.

Identity

The theme of identity also plays a large role in *The Westing Game*. Throughout the novel, many of the characters go to great lengths to obscure their true identities. For instance, Windy Windkloppel, the actual name of Samuel Westing, uses four different identities - Barney Northup, Sandy McSouthers, Julian Eastman, and Samuel Westing - to hide his true motives and intentions. Moreover, Otis Amber, the delivery boy in the novel and one of the Westing heirs, frequently conceals his identity in the novel by acting as if he is unintelligent and foolish throughout the novel. However, it is later revealed that Otis Amber only acted as if he was ignorant to shroud his true identity as a private investigator.

While some of the characters hide their identities in *The Westing Game* to avoid suspicion, other characters actually struggle to decipher their real identities as a human being. Angela Wexler, the daughter of Grace and Jake Wexler, does not have an identity for most of the novel as she is simply known as the beautiful girl marrying the intelligent intern, Denton Deere. It is only later in the novel when Angela leaves Denton and pursues a career in the medical field that she begins to find her own identity. Additionally, James Shin Hoo struggles with his own cultural identity. In Chapter 17, J.J. Ford discovers that James Hoo only added Shin to his name when he went into the restaurant business because he wanted to sound more Chinese. Hoo does not feel secure in his own identity as a Chinese man, and it is apparent that he feels the need to lie about his identity to ensure success in the restaurant business.

Regret

The entire scheme of the Westing game revolves around one man's regrets from his past and his desire to rectify past mistakes. Sam Westing's personal wrongs with his wife are ultimately the driving factor for why he brings all of the participants together. In his old age, he wants to help her move on after his regret over his role over Violet's death as a type of penance for past sins. The ability to help out all the others who are connected to his daughter gives him a sense of penance that the former Mrs. Westing seeks.

Crow's work at the soup kitchen mirrors a similar form of regret and penance. For her perceived role in her daughter's death, Crow serves soup to the poor and clings to her Christian faith to cope. Ultimately the penance of the Westing game allows for her to take the money she would have never taken from her husband and put it towards the soup kitchen.

Class

In a book where so much of the plot revolves around money, the characters are often defined by who can and who cannot afford things. The obstacle for multiple characters between achieving and not achieving their goals depends on the money from the Westing game. Characters like Angela and Theo both want to pursue their education but cannot (Angela can't because of her parents' financial issues, and Theo can't because of his brother's disease). The constraints of their class keep them from following their dreams, but the game provides an opportunity to overcome that.

J.J. Ford overcomes her class as the daughter of one of Sam Westing's staff mostly on her own, but it is revealed that Sam Westing gave her a loan in order to go to school. This generosity enables her to go on and rise up to become a judge and rise to a new class. To Sam Westing, money should be a motivator to empower the players of the game to better their lives themselves, rather than something to live off of.

The Westing Game Quotes and Analysis

Then one day (it happened to be the Fourth of July), a most uncommon-looking delivery boy rode around town slipping letters under the doors of the chosen tenants-to-be. The delivery boy was sixty-two years old, and there was no such person as Barney Northup.

Narrator, Chapter 1

At the beginning of *The Westing Game*, the reader is immediately introduced to one of the main themes of *The Westing Game*: lies and deception. Barney Northup, the aforementioned delivery boy, is the first character that the reader meets in the novel, and he formally shows apartments within Sunset Towers to the 16 chosen tenants, who are also known as the Westing heirs. However, Barney's presence within the opening scenes of the novel is complicated by the fact that he is not exactly forthcoming about his true identity; he convinces the 16 Westing heirs that they should rent an apartment as it will fit each of their needs, but he is actually acting as a pawn within the much larger confines of the novel. Although Barney does not make many more appearances throughout the novel other than the first chapter, his character acts as a catalyst for the mystery and deception that Ellen Raskin utilizes in the novel. Barney's character forces the reader to question the real motives of each individual character in the novel, and he even creates an aura of unease in the heart of the reader that travels throughout the entire novel.

A dressmaker, a secretary, an inventor, a doctor, a judge. And, oh yes, one was a bookie, one was a burglar, one was a bomber, and one was a mistake. Barney Northup had rented one of the apartments to the wrong person.

Narrator, Chapter 1

At the end of chapter one, Ellen Raskin provides the reader with various characteristics and professions of some of the Westing Hheirs, who are the 16 tenants living in Sunset Towers. Initially, the job titles/characteristics seem normal and reasonable, as Raskin creates the illusion that regular, ordinary people live in Sunset Towers. Conversely, the mood changes drastically when Raskin notes that a few of the tenants living in Sunset Towers are characters with rather questionable backgrounds such as the burglar and the bomber. By stating the hidden characteristics of some of the tenants, Raskin immediately creates various red herrings that the reader will feel obligated to discover and eliminate as the novel progresses. Also, Raskin crafts a sense of intrigue by making the reader evaluate the backgrounds of the Westing heirs in order to discover their true identities.

"Oh, it's you." Mrs. Wexler always seemed surprised to see her other daughter, so unlike golden-haired, angel-faced Angela.

Grace Wexler, Chapter 3

From the beginning of *The Westing Game*, it is made clear that even though there are 16 distinct characters within the novel, Turtle Wexler, a sassy but intelligent 13-year-old girl, is the main character of the book. Due to her distinction as the main character, Ellen Raskin focuses heavily on the interactions between Turtle and her family members--especially the relationship between Turtle and her mother, Grace Wexler. Throughout the novel, it is apparent that Grace Wexler favors her older, more attractive daughter, Angela, compared to Turtle. This causes Grace to view Turtle's rebellious antics with disdain and hatred. Grace's quote in chapter three showcases how she views Turtle with contempt even when Turtle is simply entering the room. Grace's constant comparisons often make Turtle feel unwanted and undesired, which have a much larger impact over the course of the novel.

A great patriot, Samuel Westing was famous for his fun-filled Fourth of July celebrations. Whether disguised as Ben Franklin or a lowly drummer boy, he always acted a role in the elaborately staged pageants which he wrote and directed. Perhaps best remembered was his surprise portrayal of Betsy Ross.

Narrator, Chapter 4

After the Westing heirs discover that Samuel Westing has died in chapter four, an obituary for the rich businessman appears in the local newspaper. The newspaper says that Samuel Westing not only loved celebrating Fourth of July, but he also enjoyed disguising himself in complex manners for his various celebrations. Although this line seems like a throwaway line at the beginning of the novel, it has greater importance as the reader progresses through *The Westing Game.* With Westing's death, Raskin creates a diversion that causes the reader to believe that Westing has actually died. However, after the middle of the novel, it becomes clear that Samuel Westing is not dead; in fact, it becomes apparent that Samuel Westing has disguised himself once again, and he has been participating in the Westing Game throughout the entire novel.

Some are not who they say they are, and some are not who they seem to be.

Samuel Westing, Chapter 7

In chapter seven, the Westing heirs are placed into teams of two, and then they are presented clues from a presumably dead Samuel Westing. As Westing's lawyer, Edgar Plum, is reading the clues, he notes that "Some are not who they say they are, and some are not who they seem to be." The quote works within the theme of lies and deception within the novel, but it also forces the reader to question the true identities of the characters in *The Westing Game.* Even in the novel, each character begins to wonder about the true identity of his or her counterpart. For instance, many of the characters accuse each other of being Samuel Westing's murderer throughout the novel, thus creating multiple red herrings over the course of the novel.

Why bother with driving lessons, her mother said, anyone as pretty as you can always find a handsome young man to chauffeur you. She should have insisted. She should have said no just one to her mother, just once. It was too late now.

Angela Wexler, Chapter 14

Throughout *The Westing Game,* it is evident that Angela Wexler is submissive to her mother, Grace Wexler, and her wishes. Even though Angela is 20 years old and a fully functioning adult, she barely thinks for herself for most of the novel. Angela allows Grace to make many of her choices for her, which include encouraging Angela to marry Denton Deere, a young intern, despite her obvious dislike for Deere, as well as not allowing Angela to learn how to drive because of her beauty. Grace's treatment of Angela unfortunately forces her to become dependent on the people around her to survive; Angela cannot complete everyday tasks because she has been pampered and treated as if she is a helpless princess. Angela's reluctance to speak up for herself has placed her into social situations where she cannot survive or prosper-- even as an adult.

It can have no bearing on the matter before us. Sam Westing manipulated people, cheated workers, bribed officials, stole ideas, but Sam Westing never smoked or drank or placed a bet. Give me a bookie any day over such a fine, upstanding, clean-living man.

J.J. Ford, Chapter 19

In a conversation with Sandy McSouthers, later revealed to be Samuel Westing in disguise, J.J. Ford learns that Jake Wexler, the father of Angela and Turtle Wexler, is a bookie. While Sandy seems to argue that Jake has questionable morals because of his status as a bookie, J.J. Ford quickly rebukes Sandy by noting that even though Sam did not give into vices such as gambling or drinking, he still swindled those around him in order to succeed in the world. Ford's statement showcases that while Sam Westing perceived himself to be a pillar of morality, he was still a liar and a manipulator, which puts him in the same category as those who have immoral job titles.

Angela could not be the bomber, not that sweet, pretty thing. Thing? Is that how she regarded that young woman, as a thing? And what had she ever said to her except "I hear you're getting married, Angela" or "How pretty you look, Angela." Had anyone asked about her ideas, her hopes, her plans? If I had been treated like that I'd have used dynamite, not fireworks; no, I would have just walked out and kept right on going. But Angela was different.

In chapter twenty-one, Turtle Wexler reveals that Angela Wexler, her sister, has been responsible for the bombings that have occurred in Sunset Towers. Initially, J.J. Ford cannot believe that someone as sweet and perfect as Angela could have completed the bombings. However, J.J. Ford realizes that Angela has not truly been treated as if she is an actual human being during the Westing Game. When people talk to Angela in the novel, they only focus on her beauty or her wedding to Denton Deere--no one takes the time to understand the complexities of Angela as a human being, who has real dreams and goals like everyone else. J.J. Ford's realization of Angela's complexities signal the beginning of a shift in the novel where people start to treat Angela like a real person as opposed to a "thing" with no emotions, motivations, etc.

"Hi there, Alice," T. R. Wexler said. "Ready for a game of chess?"

T.R. Wexler, Chapter 20

The final lines of the novel convey that the adult Turtle Wexler is passing on the skills taught to her by chess master Sam Westing down through her family. The things Sam Westing taught her (from the stock market to chess) will likely live on through the Wexler family.

America! America! God shed His grace on thee And crown thy good with brotherhood From sea to shining sea!

Sam Westing's clues

Why does Sam Westing choose this song as the vessel for his clues? Ultimately this story celebrates what makes America great. This novel touches on the diversity of the country, as demonstrated by the cast of characters in Sunset Tower, and shows how even a poor man like Sam Westing can become a millionaire. The point of the Westing Game was to bond together the group of people whose lives Sam Westing had touched, and the clue was in the song to shed grace and spread brotherhood.

The Westing Game Chapter 1 (Sunset Towers) - Chapter 7 (The Westing Game) Summary and Analysis

Summary

The book opens with a strange building: Sunset Towers. Sunset Towers faces east, despite the fact that the sun sets in the west, and had no towers to speak of. It stands entirely unoccupied on Lake Michigan. A 62-year-old man delivers a letter inviting six people (only six) to come live in the apartment building for a once-in-a-lifetime opportunity. There is also an opportunity to rent a doctor's office in the lobby, a coffee shop, and a restaurant on the top floor. Each letter is signed by "Barney Northrup" but the narrator clues us in that there is no such person.

The first family to view the apartments are the Wexlers. Barney Northrup shows the apartments with expertise and Grace Wexler is overjoyed with the apartment (though her husband Dr. Jake Wexler feels otherwise) and they decide to buy. Sydelle Pulaski, a secretary, is less impressed, though she decides to take it. The apartments view the Westing Estate in the distance.

On one day, all of the apartments are rented as follows:

Office: Dr. Wexler
Lobby: Theodorakis Coffee Shop
2C: F. Baumbach
2D: Theodorakis
3C: S. Pulaski
3D: Wexler
4C: Hoo
4D: J.J. Ford
5: Shin Hoo's Restaurant

We are warned that Barney Northrup rented one apartment to the wrong person.

On September 1, all the tenants move in. There is little sense of community in Sunset Towers, but it is cordial. The youngest tenants - Doug Hoo, Theo Theodorakis, and Turtle Wexler - all discuss the mysterious happenings at the Westing Mansion with the 62-year-old delivery boy, Otis Amber, and the stocky doorman, Sandy McSouthers. Otis tells the spooky tale of an unfortunate fellow who went into the mansion, and came out screaming, chased by a ghost - or worse, yelling about "purple waves." While they discuss the happenings, they see that there is smoke coming from the Westing House chimney, watched by Theo's handicapped brother, Chris, who earlier in the day had seen someone come out of the Westing house.

Days later, Angela Wexler is being fitted for her wedding gown by Flora Baumbach, who is a local dressmaker who lives in the building. She is supervised by her overbearing mother, Grace. Turtle enters the apartment and tells them all about the smoke rising from the Westing Apartment. She is dismissed by her mother, but Angela and Flora listen with interest.

Downstairs in Turtle's father's office, Dr. Wexler cuts a corn off of the foot of Mrs. Crow, who notices the smoke in the window as well. She repeats the rumor that Sam Westing's corpse must be rotting away in his mansion on an Oriental rug.

Mr. Hoo simmers about his restaurant's lack of business and greets the return of Sam Westing with contempt, implying that they have a history. He takes out his frustrations on his son, who he forces to study.

Judge J.J. Ford returns home to Sunset Towers and asks Sandy McSouthers for her thoughts about the return of Sam Westing, repeating what he's heard from Otis Amber. The judge insults her, then thinks of her position as the first black female judge in the state and retracts her insult. She considers how, if Sam Westing is truly back, she will pay him back and if he will accept it.

Chris doesn't tell his brother Theo about the mysterious figure with the limp who he saw go into the Westing House and instead allows Theo to tell him the scary story about a corpse on the Oriental rug. Sydelle Pulaski always says that he has a "smile that could break your heart."

Sydelle Pulaski feels like no one notices her, but she plots a way to never be overlooked again. Her plot involves crutches, paint thinner, paint, and brushes.

On Halloween, Turtle Wexler dresses as a witch and ascends to the Westing House, fully stocked to spend the night there at the rate of two dollars for every minute she spends inside. She surprises them by actually following through with the feat—she stays inside for twelve minutes before coming out screaming. She claims she saw the dead body of Sam Westing lying in a four-poster bed, while a voice repeated "purple waves" over and over before she ran away.

The next day, the daily newspaper reports Sam Westing is dead. He was born poor and built his fortune in the company Westing Paper Products. A spokesman for the head of the company, Julian Eastman, makes a statement about the tragedy.

Otis Amber then delivers letters to every single resident of Sunset Towers, asking for their presence the next day at 4 p.m. for a reading of Sam Westing's will. Everyone is mystified by who could possibly be related to Sam Westing.

The next day each of the tenants gathers at the Westing House. Most tenants have not been together in a room before, so awkwardness ensues. Flora coos to Chris, and is told off by Theo for treating her brother like he's a baby or retarded. Grace Wexler wears furs to show she is not a poor relative and shakes J.J. Ford's hand to show that she is liberal enough to shake hands with a black woman.

The lawyer handling the case is E. J. Plum, a young inexperienced lawyer who Judge Ford remembers as incompetent. Before they get started, Sydelle arrives on crutches. She claims that she has a wasting disease that will kill her slowly, clearly enjoying the attention. On her dress, she wears purple waves.

E.J. Plum begins the reading of the will, reminding the crowd that he has never met Sam Westing. The will is separated into 11 parts. The FIRST claims that each person in the racially diverse crowd is one of his 16 nieces and nephews, causing outrage from Grace Windsor Wexler that he miraculously predicts. The SECOND claims that he was murdered by someone in the room, which causes another outcry. The THIRD asks who among them is worthy to be the heir. The FOURTH says they too may strike it rich if they choose to play the Westing Game. The FIFTH correctly predicts an interruption from Judge Ford. The SIXTH asks for a minute of silence for Uncle Sam. They move into the game room for the rest of the will where eight card tables wait for them. The SEVENTH part explains the rules:

- *Number of players: 16, divided into 8 pairs.*
- *Each pair will receive $10,000.*
- *Each pair will receive one set of clues.*
- *Forfeits: If any player drops out, the partner must leave the game. The pair must return the money. Absent pairs forfeit the $10,000; their clues will be held until the next session.*
- *Players will be given two days' notice of the next session. Each pair may then give one answer.*
- *Object of the game: to win.*

The pairs are as follows:

MADAME SUN LIN HOO, *cook*
JAKE WEXLER, *standing or sitting* when not lying down
(Both of these partners are not present, disqualifying them)

TURTLE WEXLER, *witch,*
FLORA BAUMBACH, *dressmaker*

CHRISTOS THEODORAKIS, *birdwatcher*
D. DENTON DEERE, intern, St. Joseph's Hospital, Department of Plastic Surgery

ALEXANDER MCSOUTHERS, *doorman*
J. J. FORD, *judge, Appellate Division of the State Supreme Court*

GRACE WINDSOR WEXLER, *heiress*
JAMES SHIN HOO, *restaurateur*

BERTHE ERICA CROW, *Good Salvation Soup Kitchen*
OTIS AMBER, *deliverer*

THEO THEODORAKIS, *brother*
DOUG HOO, *first in all-state high-school mile run*

SYDELLE PULASKI, *secretary to the president*
ANGELA WEXLER, none

NINTH, each pair receives a check for $10,000. And TENTH, each pair receives a pair of different clues. Everyone reacts differently to their clues, most strongly Judge Ford, who accuses the clues of having a racially insensitive tinge. Finally, the ELEVENTH closes with a warning that not everyone is who they say they are. If they know who they are, and what they want, and which way the wind blows, they will be successful. If they do not, they will fail.

Analysis

The Westing Game sets up the elements of a classic murder mystery. The characters each have something to hide and something to gain by the death of Sam Westing, but Raskin augments the story with a twist: Sam Westing will reward the one who solves the mystery of who killed him. This two-part, murder-mystery game setup creates a unique story engine.

The setup of who lives in Sunset Towers so close to the Westing Mansion seems planned by an omniscient force. The mysterious Barney Northum follows orders to get a specific group of seemingly unconnected people into one place. Whoever he is, he is exceptionally good at convincing the future tenants that this is where they belong. Nothing is up to chance or fate; it's all by design.

The story does not seem to revolve around one particular character as a protagonist; we are given glimpses into the minds of each character through the lens of an omniscient narrator. The reader can jump from apartment to apartment and is given a sense that they know more than the characters, though not the identity of the murderer.

One element that Raskin clearly wants to highlight is the diversity of the characters. In the cast we have Greek, Chinese, black, disabled, Jewish, and Polish characters, a deliberate choice for its publication in 1978. These identities are not unconnected to the plot; they can be a point of tension for the characters and fuel their motivations. The willingness to tackle these themes show that even though classified as a children's book, *The Westing Game* is ahead of its time.

Also, even though it's a children's book, there are glimmers of adult humor. When Dr. Wexler is asked to record his position, he replies "standing up when not lying down," which could go over the head of younger readers. She also shows she is unafraid of skewering social satire, as she paints Grace Wexler as a social-climbing housewife with a complete lack of self-awareness. In fact, it is the children in the story who seem to have the best grasp on the ways of the world, surrounded by ridiculous and at times nasty adults.

The Westing Game Chapter 8 (The Paired Heirs) - Chapter 10 (The Westing Game) Summary and Analysis

Summary

That night a massive snowstorm hits Sunset Towers. The tenants wake up to no electricity. Turtle Wexler takes advantage of the situation and sells emergency candles to the tenants at the inflated rate of $5 each.

Each of the pairs wastes no time. Sydelle is the most popular tenant in Sunset Towers because as a secretary, she is the only one who bothered to transcribe the will. Angela and Sydelle become a dynamic duo, and begin to go around the complex asking about clues. They start with Chris, the partner of Angela's finance. He reveals that he is looking for grains. In his clue ("FOR PLAIN GRAIN SEED") he unscrambles the name "FORD" and gets Otis Amber from oats, a kind of grain.

Flora and Turtle take their clue "SEA MOUNTAIN AM O" and speculate that the quote "Take stock in America" and "go for broke" in the will suggest they should invest their $10,000 in the stock market.

Mr. Hoo and Grace Wexler are trying to decipher "FRUITED PURPLE WAVES FOR SEA." Grace makes a racist comment about it being difficult to tell the ages of Oriental people, and makes it worse by suggesting that the murderer lives in 4C ("FOR SEA"), which is where Mr. Hoo lives. They both get in a fight and stop working.

Doug and Theo have trouble with their clues ("HIS N ON TO THEE FOR"). Theo reveals he was playing chess with someone in the game room last night, but doesn't remember who.

Judge Ford reads her clue ("SKIES AM SHINING BROTHER") and considers the letter signed by Samuel Sykes that says that Westing was sane. She considers the fact that perhaps Sam Westing was trying to use this game to frame someone who he had history with and was trapping the players with greed to get revenge. She vows to find out as much as she can about each of the players to protect them. She calls the newspaper and asks for them to supply information about each of the players.

Angela and Sydelle look through their five clues: "GOOD, HOOD, FROM, SPACIOUS, GRACE." They also have the clues that they overheard from the other night at the Westing Mansion: "KING, QUEEN" from Otis Amber, "PURPLE WAVES" overheard from Grace, "ON" or "NO" overheard from Doug and Theo, and "GRAINS" from Chris. They also have all the info from Turtle's stock market exploits that they found crumpled on a piece of paper (500 shares of MT). Altogether the clues read"

"GOOD HOOD FROM SPACIOUS GRACE KING QUEEN PURPLE WAVES ON (NO) GRAINS MOUNTAIN (EMPTY)"

Theo enters and asks if either of them is interested in playing chess. Both Sydelle an Angela refuse, but realize that Sam Westing is a chess master. Sydelle repeats from the will "object of the game: to win" but Angela mishears it as "object of the game: twin." They then decide to find out who in the apartments could possibly be a twin. Sydelle discovers when she returns to her apartment that someone has stolen her notebook that she transcribed the will in.

Sydelle creates a bulletin board in the elevator asking for her business papers to be returned, and it becomes a hit in the apartment. People begin posting non-stop about missing items, rewards, and advertisements for their services. Judge Ford posts that she is having a party at her apartment that evening.

Before the party, Turtle returns home to her apartment where her mother tries to flatter her for the first time, calling her "pretty" and other words typically reserved for Angela. She then tries to get her to reveal some of her clues, to which Turtle refuses. Angela and Sydelle arrive, and Grace turns her attention to attempting to get them to give her their clues. They refuse, but the two of them are dressed identically as twins in an attempt to figure out if there is a twin in their midst. Grace tells Sydelle that if she wins the inheritance, everything she owns will go to Angela, which hurts Turtle's feelings.

Judge Ford is given information about the following people from the newspapers. Angela and D. Denton Deere had an engagement announcement. James Hoo had brought a lawsuit against Mr. Westing for claiming he stole his idea for disposable diapers. Doug Hoo ran one of the fastest miles in Wisconsin.

The party begins, and Grace Wexler is the first one to arrive with her husband. Judge Ford talks to them, but after asking how Grace is related to Sam Westing she dismisses her as a "prattling pretender." No one is particularly successful at getting clues. Sydelle fails to learn if anyone is a twin and generally Angela feels that all anyone wants to talk about with her are her impending nuptials. She feels as though that's all anyone knows about her. Judge Ford watches the guests interact. For the first time, we meet George and Catherine Theodorakis who are not a part of the Westing Game. Turtle decides to take a poll about the line "may God thy gold refine" and whether it came from Shakespeare or the Bible. The only one to remember the quote in full is Sydelle Pulaski, who remembers "spend it wisely and may God thy gold refine." There is no clue that comes out of it, and the guests return home a little dejected.

Analysis

In this section of the book, we see that the pairs each work together well in their own way. After being isolated from each other, the tenants of Sunset Towers are now spending time together. The clues are confusing, but they are bringing the complex together.

The first pair worth noting is Flora and Turtle. Turtle, who has been hungry for maternal love, now has a person who trusts her opinion and respects her. Turtle seems to be the most creative, thinking outside the box about what the clues could mean. Her idea to enter the stock market does not seem to be paying dividends yet, but could soon.

A character who has more information than he is letting on is Chris Theodorakis. The identity of the limping figure who enters the Westing House is still unknown to both the reader and presumably Theo and Chris as well.

A pair that seems to be getting on surprisingly well is Grace and Mr. Hoo. Though it seems they had little to no personal ties before, they seem perfectly willing to call out one another and be frank and truthful. Mr. Hoo seems to be someone with a reason to dislike Mr. Westing.

Sydelle seems to finally be getting the attention she's been craving. Having such a beautiful partner in Grace Wexler seems to have boosted her confidence and the fact that she is the keeper of the transcription of the will has made her suddenly the center of attention. The irony is, the Westing Game is making people notice her, not her actual injury.

At this point in the novel, Judge J.J. Ford seems to be going at the Westing Game alone. While her partner Sandy McSouthers seems largely absent, she is taking on an investigative role. Her decision to call the newspapers shows that no one's past is safe. As a character who seems to have history with Sam Westing, she comes up with the theory that he is simply using the Westing Game to frame someone who he himself had a grudge against, furthering the theory that in the Westing Game, nothing is as it seems.

The Westing Game Chapter 11 (The Meeting) - Chapter 15 (Fact and Gossip) Summary and Analysis

Summary

The big debate among the tenants of the apartment now is whether or not to collaborate with other teams. Both Turtle and Flora make discoveries about their respective partners. Turtle finds out that Flora had a daughter, but she's gone. Flora finds out that Turtle's real name is in fact Tabatha Ruth.

In the Theodorakis' coffee shop, Theo and Doug call a meeting to ask Grace, Sydelle, Angela, and Mr. Hoo if anyone's clues make any sense to them, and then asks them if anyone wants to play in a chess tournament. Mr. Hoo reveals that he has found Sydelle's transcription of the will, which she reveals is useless to anyone besides her since she transcribed it in Polish.

The group agrees to give Sydelle a larger share of the inheritance in exchange for her notes (in English). Mr. Hoo offers to share his clues to prove that he and Grace Wexler are innocent. Instead, Judge Ford suggests that since everyone is innocent until proven guilty, they should not share clues and are allowed to ask anonymous questions instead.

"Is anyone here a twin?" No one answers.

"What is Turtle's real name?" Grace Wexler lies and Flora tells the truth.

"How many people here have actually met Sam Westing?" Only Mr. Hoo.

"Who got kicked last week?" No answer.

Suddenly, there's an explosion. Everyone in the restaurant thinks they're covered in blood, but they realize it's tomato sauce. George Theodorakis concludes that it's a bomb. His wife Catherine agrees.

In Sydelle's apartment, Turtle tells Angela that their mother thinks Angela stole Sydelle's notebook. Turtle then says that she doesn't think Angela wants to marry her fiancee. Sydelle says that Turtle is jealous, and she retorts that at least she doesn't need a crutch to get attention. Sydelle snaps back that Turtle's crutch is her big mouth, but Angela thinks that her crutch is her braid.

The newspaperman calls up Judge Ford to inform her that George Theodorakis at one point escorted Violet Westing to a party in Westingtown. She now knows that Mr. Hoo, George, Sandy, and herself all know Sam Westing. She decides to call a private investigator, but to her surprise, when he picks up the phone, that person shares the same voice as Sam Westing.

A second bomb is planted Shin Hoo's restaurant, placed specifically with a candle to react with MSG. Grace Wexler assists Shin Hoo in the restaurant and decides to play matchmaker with the couples. She wheels Chris over to dine with Sydelle and they get on famously. Angela begins talking to Theo about their mutual desire to go to college, and how they both can't: Theo because of the cost of the operation for Chris, and Angela because of her engagement and family troubles. Theo reveals that he wanted to be a writer and asks Angela if she would go to college if she won the inheritance. She can't answer the question.

Judge Ford meets with Flora and discovers that she at one time made a dress for Sam Westing's daughter, Violet Westing. In Hoo's restaurant, Jake Wexler is jealous of his wife's chumminess with Mr. Hoo and Turtle listens to the stock market (down 12 points!) on a radio. Chris and Sydelle bond and she accuses him of being the murderer, which pleases him. Sydelle gets up to give her compliments to the chef and goes into the kitchen just as Otis Amber arrives. The bomb goes off. Only Sydelle is injured, and she is taken to the hospital.

Finally, the snow melts and the tenants of Sunset Tower are freed. Angela looks under the hoods of cars in answer to the clues "Good gracious from hood space." Flora takes Turtle to a broker's office to check on the status of their investments. They are not doing well.

Judge Ford tries to tip Sandy, who refuses because she gave him the entirety of the $10,000. He tries to help with the clues, identifying Dr. Sikes, Otis Amber, Mr. Hoo, and Theo or Chris as potential suspects. She suggests that perhaps Sam Westing is out to get one of the people on the list.

Grace and Mr. Hoo argue about whether or not to start an advertising campaign for the restaurant as Crow and Otis Amber reminisce about an unarmed person. Otis Amber mutters to himself that so many people are buying Westing Paper Products that it's messing up his deliveries.

Denton Deere explains to Chris that he is a plastic surgery intern and can't help with his condition. Chris tells him about the connection between Judge Ford living in Apt 4D. He refuses to cosign the check.

While Angela waits for Denton, Theo arrives in the lobby. He finds the answer to where the phrase "May God thy gold refine" comes from: "America, the Beautiful." Denton arrives and Theo asks if he wants to play chess. He ignores Theo, and Sandy begins whistling "America, the Beautiful."

At the hospital, Denton and Angela argue about Sydelle being crazy until a psychiatrist comes in and confirms that she made up her disease, but is not crazy. Angela visits with Sydelle and finds her without makeup or her usual unctuous air. While Angela looks for her makeup, she finds a strange letter asking for forgiveness in a "tense rigid hand." At the bottom are the clues "Thy Beautiful."

Things start to return to normal at Sunset Towers. Both the coffee shop and restaurant reopen, and people return to their normal schedules. Turtle and Flora continue to lose money on the stock market.

Doug, Turtle, and Otis commiserate about how Westing could've died since Turtle claimed he looked too peaceful to have been murdered. Doug suggests that perhaps someone injected him with bee or snake venom. Doug then mentions that he saw someone in Turtle's red boots looking through the hoods of the cars that morning, before running away. Otis Amber claims he doesn't believe the murder actually happened. Turtle speaks to Sandy about whether anyone besides her left Sunset Towers on Halloween night. He remembers that both Otis and Crow also left. He then tells her a parable about a man who had his death predicted for him, but when it never came, he laughed. He died laughing.

Jake visits his wife at Hoo's restaurant. Hoo and Grace argue about a potential advertising campaign involving renaming the restaurant "Hoo's on First" after the old comedy routine. Mr. Hoo hates it, but Jake pretends to like it to appease his wife.

Judge Ford discovers that Sam Westing's wife was a thin, shy woman who seemed to hate the limelight and that his daughter Violet was engaged to a senator who is now in jail for bribery. The rumor was, according to Sandy, that she killed herself rather than marry the politician. The parallel between Violet looking like Angela and her being involved with Theo's father is not lost on them, and Sandy says if the scenario was to play out like it did in the past that Angela Wexler would have to die.

Analysis

The Sunset Towers community is coming together to solve the clues, but they are not making much progress. Rather than discovering clues related to the murders, they are discovering facts about each other. Now, partnerships are branching out to seek help from other pairs.

The Westing Game is turning surprisingly dangerous. Not one but two bombs have gone off in the building: one simply spraying tomato sauce everywhere, the other injuring Sydelle. The is a sense of foreboding that there will likely be another bomb and that it will be more serious than the previous two.

The characters get close enough that they can speak candidly with each other. Turtle calls out her sister for not really wanting to marry Denton and Sydelle observes that she's jealous. Turtle is then comfortable enough to accuse Sydelle of making up her injury, which is of course confirmed by the psychiatrist after she ironically is truly injured by the bomb. Accusations get more personal as the cloud of suspicion descends over each of them.

Grace tries her hand at playing matchmaker. There is undeniable chemistry between Theo and Angela, who is feeling as though most of her decisions are being made for her. The discovery that both she and Theo had to turn down college for their families bonds them together. Surprisingly, Chris and Sydelle communicate extremely well and have a similar chemistry that keeps them laughing all through their dinner.

Ford continues to rely on the information from the papers. She learns the sad history of the Westing family and how other tenant's stories are intertwined. Flora made the ill-fated wedding gown for his daughter Violet. Theo's father used to be a suitor. Sandy remembers Mrs. Westing with a mole, whereas Judge Ford does not. It seems that either the investigator is misleading them or Sandy is misremembering. Judge Ford also believes that perhaps what Sam Westing is truly after is revenge from his grave.

The Westing Game Chapter 16 (The Third Bomb) - Chapter 21 (The Fourth Bomb) Summary and Analysis

Summary

The women of Sunset Towers watch as Angela opens her presents at her bridal shower, being led by Grace Wexler. Grace orders Angela to read every card out loud. After opening a mysterious present from "Cookie Barfspringer" and two asparagus cookers, she opens a present that turns out to be the third bomb.

As the police investigate, the paranoia of the tenants grows. One of them is a bomber, a murderer, or a thief, they think as they analyze what everyone says to the police.

Turtle goes to visit her sister in the hospital. Turtle feels as through her sister prevented her from being hurt by the bomb since she pulled the present away as Turtle tried to open it for her. Turtle says that Angela will have a scar and that Angela will test her theory that being pretty isn't important. Angela wonders if this will be the case. Sydelle, who is in the hospital bed down the ward, mishears her and thinks that Angela admits to being the bomber.

Packages begin being inspected in the building as people are on high alert. Jake Wexler begins sending gifts to his wife (chocolates, long-stemmed roses), but she is very suspicious. Even Turtle saying Mrs. Baumbach's name to notify her about the falling stock market sounds like she's saying bomb and causes people stress.

Grace and Mr. Hoo begin to break down their clues as Jake and Mrs. Hoo work on her English. They decide to share clues. "Purple waves for fruited sea" becomes "Plum" which reminds them that the lawyer's name is Plum. Ed Plum. Fruit/Ed.

Sandy and Judge Ford begin compiling information about the heirs. They detail information about the Hoo family. Mr. Hoo's wife died five years ago. He apparently married his new wife for her sauce. Doug Hoo is competing in a track meet against college kids. Hoo once sued Sam Westing over stealing his design for a disposable paper diaper. The case was settled. Mr. Hoo has now invented paper innersoles, and Sandy takes credit for giving him the idea.

Theo breaks down his clues and realizes that it makes a chemical name $NH4NO3$ and reveals the murderer to be Otis. Theo runs to tell Doug, but runs into Crow instead. In a surreal moment, she pulls him into a room to pray for deliverance and gives him a letter.

The next day as Flora braids Turtle's hair, she reads the *Wall Street Journal* and updates her on the stock market. She asks if she can call her Mrs. Baba instead of Baumbach (because of the bomb scare) and they settle on Baba. Turtle asks Baba if her daughter Rosalie was smart, and she replies that Turtle is the smartest child she's ever met. Turtle gets jealous, however, when Flora begins talking about her daughter again.

Sandy collects information on Flora. We learn that Rosalie was Mrs. Baumbach's mentally handicap daughter who died of pneumonia at the age of 19. Flora also made a gown for Violet Westing. He then reads the file on Otis Amber and almost falls out of his chair from laughing so hard.

Theo is unsure about whether or not the night's event with Crow was a dream or not. He tells Doug that he thinks he's figured out the clues and asks him to follow Otis Amber.

Flora watches as the stock for Westing Paper Products climbs and climbs.

Doug follows Otis Amber all over town, seriously blistering his feet in the process. Eventually, after Otis catches him, he reveals that he's been given letters from Ed Plum, who wants them all to meet at the Westing House that Saturday night.

Sandy and Judge Ford meet and read the dossiers on the remaining heirs. Otis Amber is a 62-year-old fourth grade dropout with an IQ of 50 with no relatives. His connection to Westing is that delivers mail for E.J. Plum. Regarding Denton Deere, they learn he is a graduate of UW Madison. His connection to Westing is that he is engaged to Angela, who looks like his daughter. For Sydelle, they learn that she is secretary to the president of Schultz Sausages and had likely been faking her injury. She has no known Westing connection.

In the hospital, Angela refuses to have plastic surgery to hide her scar, despite the insistence of Denton. Turtle arrives and warns Angela not to say anything to anyone after learning she changed her position on the letter to "person." Ed Plum arrives to speak to Angela, and when Grace arrives and sees him standing over Angela, she shrieks (thinking he's the murderer).

Chris has three visitors in one day. One is Otis Amber to deliver the letter. The second is Flora to give him a clue because she felt guilty that she read one of his dropped ones. Finally, Denton arrives and tells him he knows a doctor that may be able to help him with his condition.

Flora listens in delight as their stock climbs to $46 a share. Turtle is getting in trouble at school because she is constantly inventing medical maladies to excuse her listening to the radio every 30 minutes. The toothaches and bladder infections, however, do not convince the school doctors.

Crow polishes silver in the Wexler's apartment, when Otis arrives and confesses that he believes that Mr. Hoo is the bomber. Crow vows vengeance that he injured and scarred Angela.

Judge Ford and Sandy pull up the file on Berthe Erica Crow. She was married at 16 to a man named Windy Windkloppel and divorced at 40. She used to be an alcoholic, but ultimately gave it up when she found God. She has no known connection to Sam Westing.

Crow visits Hoo's restaurant where now Jake and Mrs. Hoo are flirting. This time, Grace is jealous. Crow is determined to have revenge on the bomber, Hoo, but when she sees Jake, she complains about the pain in her toes. Mr. Hoo jumps in and gives her a paper innersole that he invented, which makes her change her mind completely about Mr. Hoo being the bomber.

Chris arrives at the hospital and wheels to Angela's bed, where he gives her the letter that Crow gave his brother. In it, two clues are attached: "With. Majesties." Angela realizes that the clues of Crow and Otis Amber aren't king and queen after all.

Sandy complies more information on the heirs. Jake Wexler graduated from Marquette. Grace was born Gracie Windkloppel (the same surname as Crow's first husband). Angela has one year of college with good grades. Turtle plays the stock market. The connections are that Grace claims that Sam Westing is her real uncle, and Angela looks like Violet... but so does Grace, though she's older. Sandy tells the judge that Jake is a bookie, and she says that Sam Westing was much worse since he cheated and bribed, even though he had no vices.

Sandy and Ford then realize the connection between Grace's maiden name and the name of Crow's first husband. They then realize that they have that name in an interview from a Sybil Pulaski, and they realize that Sam Westing mistakenly chose Sydelle instead of Sybil.

Finally, when Westing Paper Products hits $52 a share, Turtle tells Flora to sell. Doug Hoo continues to trail Otis Amber, until he is thrown off the scent.

Theo experiments with the explosives mentioned and ends up in the emergency room. Luckily, he has an alibi which prevents him from becoming a suspect.

Judge Ford goes and interviews George Theodorakis about his relationship to Violet Westing. They were high school sweethearts, but Violet Westing's mother wanted her to marry someone with more money, so she broke it off after her mother arranged for her to marry a senator. Seeing no way out, Violet killed herself. With this, Sandy is able to complete the file on the Theodorakis family. Judge Ford begins to speculate that the person Sam Westing is targeting is the person who he hates the most: the woman who is responsible for the death of his daughter. Judge Ford speculates that perhaps Mrs. Westing is still alive, and one of the heirs.

Turtle and Flora count their money as Theo comes in and asks to borrow Turtle's bike. Turtle grudgingly acquiesces, then calls to check on Angela. When she doesn't answer, she fears that she is being interrogated for a planting a bomb. Theo tracks Crow and Otis on a bus to a seedy part of town to the Good Salvation Soup Kitchen. Theo watches them help the poor and needy, feels guilty for spying, and returns home.

Sandy completes his own heir profile, revealing that he was born in Edinburgh and was a worker in the Westing plant before being fired for trying to unionize the workers. He then completes a profile on Judge Josie-Jo Ford. She reveals that her mother was a servant to the Westings and her father worked in the gardens on their days off. She never played with Violet, but she played chess with Sam Westing, who beat her every time. She then tells Sandy that Sam Westing paid for her entire education (mostly to have a judge on his side) and she never repaid the debt.

Another bomb goes off in the elevator of Sunset Towers. However, this time the bomber is caught, as there is a sign that says "BOMBER STRIKES AGAIN" written on the back of an essay by Turtle Wexler. Grace is frantic and says she couldn't possibly be the bomber, but Judge Ford takes her into her custody for questioning.

Judge Ford warns her about the severity of what she's done, but realizes that she is probably only bombing to protect the identity of the real bomber (her sister, she suspects). Turtle then confesses what she saw on Halloween night and that Sam Westing's body looked more like a wax dummy than a dead body. Judge Ford is intrigued and gives her some bourbon to put in a cavity in Turtle's mouth. Turtle runs into Sandy who tells her she must see the dentist straight away.

At the hospital, Angela gets a note from Denton that says he loves her and also has a clue from Chris which illuminates Sydelle and Angela's clues. The clues when rearranged create the lyrics of "America The Beautiful."

Analysis

The significance of the song "America the Beautiful" has become a through line throughout the piece. The allusion to this patriotic song fits into the motif of patriotism. Sam Westing refers to himself as Uncle Sam and there is a feeling of Americaness in this mystery. The diversity of the cast helps create a portrait of America in the 1970s.

Angela is a character undergoing dynamic changes. For the first time, she feels as though she is having decisions made for her. She right now is being set up as the potential bomber, not to hurt anyone, but to take action in her own life. Her decision to change her position from "fiancee" to "person" shows the shift in her thinking.

There is a sense that perhaps some of the characters are not who they appear to be. There are holes in how a few of the characters relate to Sam Westing. One such character is Crow, who married a man with the same last name as Grace Wexler's birth surname. The similarities between the Wexler women and Violet Westing creates a suspicion that there may be a connection there.

Turtle continues to find a mother figure in Flora Baumbach. She, however, grows jealous whenever she talks about her daughter Rosalie, because she is likely tired of competing for attention with her own sister. Turtle's confession to Judge Ford is the first time she has told an adult about her experience in the mansion, increasing the likelihood that this is a clue that will solve the mystery.

There is a humorous subplot in the flirtations between the Wexlers and the Hoos. In some ways, the spouses seem more compatible with the others than with their own spouse, but this jealousy is making them pay more attention to each other. Again, it seems as one of the primary aims of the Westing Game is to get the tenants to interact more with each other.

The Westing Game Chapter 22 (Losers, Winners) - Chapter 30 (The End?) Summary and Analysis

Summary

Turtle confesses to the bombing by posting a note in the elevator. Her mother is traumatized, and Mr. Hoo tells his wife that he's lucky his son is a dumb jock. Madame Hoo considers how she'd be able to get back to China by stealing and selling Doug's track medals and Turtle's missing Mickey Mouse clock.

Grace is distraught that her daughter is the bomber, but Dr. Wexler tries to convince her to go to the track meet to cheer up. It brings up ghosts from their past - how Grace's family disowned her for marrying a Jew and how Jake feels like a loser for not being able to provide more money for his family. Turtle, Angela, and Sydelle oversee their argument and Turtle becomes upset. Jake convinces her that nothing's wrong, and they tell him that they will see them at the track meet. Angela is elated that her family is more engaged in their own problems than hers, and Angela is buoyed by the prospect that with the clue of "America the Beautiful" they will win the game.

Judge Ford believes that Sam Westing could still be alive to watch the fun and that whoever could possibly be Sam Westing's former wife (Crow, she thinks is most likely) is in terrible danger. Denton arrives with Chris, who communicates much better because of the medicine Denton has provided him with. Judge Ford reads newspaper reports that say that the car crash Sam Westing was in caused him to have to have his entire face reconstructed, which means he could look like anyone.

Turtle visits the dentist, who has a curious collection of dentures with chipped and false teeth. He fills in her cavity and she remembers Barney Northrup's visit to her parents, demanding that they pay for the damage from the bombs. She kicks him hard in the shin.

Doug Hoo wins his track meet and thanks his dad to the reporters, making both Mr. and Madame Hoo beam. Sandy McSouthers comes to Judge Ford's apartment and tells her that Barney Northrup fired him for drinking on the job. He also reveals that Otis Amber does not live in a grocer's basement and is much smarter than he lets on. He suggests that Crow is Sam Westing's ex-wife and Otis is Sam Westing. As the residents approach the Westing Mansion that night, Crow tells Otis that she feels she is in terrible danger.

As everyone arrives, they notice that Turtle has had a haircut, due to her singed braid. Everyone says she looks nice and Flora shows Turtle a picture of her deceased daughter, Rosalie. Turtle thinks about how covering up for Angela being the bomber means that her sister has to love her forever. Judge Ford arrives in a turban and robe.

The instructions this time are different, and each pair has to say something on record when their name and titles (altered to reflect how they've grown since the beginning) are called. Jake and Madam Hoo: "Boom." Flora and Turtle: "11,587.50" (their income from investing). Denton and Chris: "Mr. Westing was a good man" (he wanted them to be with the perfect partner to make friends.) Judge Ford and Sandy McSouthers: no answers, but Judge Ford sees that Otis cannot be Sam Westing. Mr. Hoo and Grace Wexler: "Ed Plum." Crow and Otis: "mother" (Crow repeating the mysterious change of title in the instructions). Doug and Theo: "no answer." Sydelle and Angela rise, and in answer, Sydelle sings two verses of "America the Beautiful" and names Otis Amber. The instructions then say there will be a short pause and calls for Crow to go to the kitchen for refreshments.

Denton says to Judge Ford that it doesn't seem as though any of the heirs have had plastic surgery, but McSouthers could've probably used some. As Sydelle and Angela badger Ed Plum for clues, he realizes he is late for reading the next clue. He opens it up and reveals the instructions: go directly to the library, do not pass go.

The next clue reveals that all answers are wrong, and that teams will be disbanded. The clue reminds them it's not what's there, it's what's missing. Ed Plum locks them in the library. Panicking, they all decide to collaborate to solve the mystery and share the inheritance. They each lay out their clues and it forms the lyrics to "America the Beautiful" with letters missing.

"O BEAUTIFUL FOR SPACIOUS SKIES FOR AM WAVES OF GRAIN FOR PURPLE MOUNTAIN MAJESTIES ABOVE FRUITED PLAIN AMERICA AM

GOD SHED HIS GRACE ON THEE
AND N THY GOOD WITH BROTHERHOOD FROM SEA TO SHINING SEA"

The missing letters are "ber," "the," "erica," and "crow" spelling out the full name Berthe Erica Crow!

Before the group can turn on Crow, Ford defends her, saying that she must be considered innocent before proven guilty and not to let their greed make them rush to conclusions. As she says this, Sandy falls to the floor clutching his throat and writhing in agony. Two men rush into the room and Dr. Sikes declares him dead. The other points out that he drank from a flask filled by Crow.

As the police arrive, Ed Plum declares that he must continue to read the will. The will declares that Samuel Westing was born Samuel "Windy" Windkloppel (the same last name as Grace's maiden name) and declares the game null and void if no one has found the murderer. They have five minutes to decide. Each person is tempted to give up the murderer, but no one does until the final minute, where Crow stands and says her own name. She says that she gives half of her $200 million inheritance to Otis for the Good Salvation Soup Kitchen, and the rest should go to Angela.

Sandy is dead. Crow is taken to jail. The remaining heirs sit in Judge Ford's living room pondering what happened. Denton accuses Turtle of kicking Sandy because he saw a bruise on Sandy's shin, but she claims she never kicked him ever and the only person she kicked was Barney Northrup. They talk about the best things about Sandy, and Theo tells the room how he used to play chess against Sandy, or at least Sandy would move the pieces in the game room when no one was watching. When Theo tells them that he took Sandy's queen, Judge Ford recognizes the classic Sam Westing move as a "queen's sacrifice." Turtle puts the pieces together and realizes that Sam Westing is Barney Northrup and Sandy, who winked at her while he was dying. Re-reading the will, she realizes that Sam Westing (Windkloppel) was the husband of Crow and their one daughter had drowned. Judge Ford agrees that maybe the point of the game was to punish Crow, or get his enemies to forgive him, as Chris suggests. Judge Ford realizes that Crow was the queen in the queen's sacrifice. Turtle stands up and starts a trial.

She says that Sam Westing and Sandy are both dead, but Crow is innocent. She questions Chris, who reveals he saw Dr. Sikes enter the Westing mansion on the night she went in. She questions Otis Amber, who reveals he is a private investigator hired by Barney Northrup, Sam Westing, and Judge Ford. He reveals Sam Westing hired him to follow his ex-wife, Crow, after she left him to make sure she stayed out of trouble. Barney Northrup hired him to investigate the heirs, as did Judge Ford. She realizes through questioning Otis that he and Sandy both cooked up the story of a dead man on the rug to entice the kids into going inside on Halloween. She then questions Denton about if Sandy really seemed dead and if the dead body could have been a wax dummy. Madame Hoo finally cannot stand the guilt and returns the things she's stolen from people in the apartment to their owners, revealing that she intended to sell them to go to China.

Turtle goes on to realize that Sam Westing must've had a fourth disguise as she remembers the quote, "The estate is at the crossroads. The heir who wins the windfall will be the one who finds the fourth." However, she does not reveal it to the group. Crow returns, interrupting the trial.

That night, a fireworks display erupts over the Westing mansion, burning the house to the ground. The only one who receives money is Crow, who receives three $10,000 checks. It seems all is lost, until Turtle goes off on her own, pursuing the man who will win her the same. She arrives at the residence of Julian Eastman, chairman of the board of Westing Paper company. It's Sam Westing. By finding him, Turtle has won the game.

She keeps the fact that he is alive secret, but visits him every Saturday afternoon. A wedding is held at Hoo's restaurant, but it's a wedding for Otis Amber and Crow. Judge Ford moves out of Sunset Towers, but not without the promise to correspond with Chris to help him get into a good college. Hoo's paper innersole gains traction. Sydelle returns to work as a secretary for Schultz's Sausages. Jake Wexler quits his practice and becomes a government official for a state inquiry into a state lottery. Grace Wexler takes over Hoo's On First and turns it into a sports-themed restaurant. Angela calls off her engagement and returns to college to study to become a doctor. Crow and Otis Amber move into the apartment above the soup kitchen, which is bolstered by Sam Westin's donation.

Five years later, the tenants reunite at the new lake-front home of the Hoo's. Doug Hoo is an Olympic medalist making his return home, as Theo who is an assistant journalist helped publish him in the papers. Sydelle becomes engaged to the president of Schultz's Sausages. Chris brings a friend, Shirley Staver. Turtle is now eighteen and in her second year of college, going by the name T.R. Wexler.

Many more years later, Sam Westing lays dying and T.R. Wexler is by his side. She is his only heir. She tells of how everyone has succeeded in life because of the Westing Game: J.J. Ford sits on the supreme court, Chris has married Shirley, Denton has married Angela, and she has married Theo. She says her goodbyes to him, having kept his secret all along. She returns home where Angela's daughter, her niece Alice, waits for her. Baba has tied ribbons in her hair and T.R. asks her if she wants to play a game of chess.

Analysis

The Westing Game is finally solved. While the premise of the book is billed as a murder mystery, it is in fact simply a mystery. There is no killer and the mystery lies in the motives of Sam Westing. The surprise twist at the end is in fact that he had no intention of harming any of the participants, but simply wished to help each and every person whose life was connected to his.

The reveal that Crow is the former Mrs. Westing ultimately is the reason for the game. He wanted her to find peace and move on with her life with the money that he could not offer her in person. Crow, who had devoted her life to finding penance for the death of Violet, was ultimately given the money necessary to continue her work at the soup kitchen and find happiness with another man who loves her, Otis Amber.

Turtle's decision to keep the real point of the game to herself shows that for her the objective of the Westing Game was never simply the money, which she learned how to invest herself, but the knowledge that she solved a puzzle, which endears her to the man who is indeed her own kin, Sam Westing. She never tells a soul, but continues to be mentored by the man who she knows as Sandy, but was Sam Westing all along.

Each of the characters goes on to find happiness as a result of the Westing Game. The game unlocks the potential in each of the characters rather than simply handing them a fortune. Angela's realization that she needs to have agency in her own life leads her to become a doctor herself before ultimately marrying Denton as an equal. Grace Wexler as well unlocks her potential as a businesswoman and becomes successful in her own right, leading her to find pride and happiness rather than fussing over her daughter.

Ultimately the Westing Game brought a diverse group of people together and made their lives better by intimately learning from those they only knew at a distance. The chess master Sam Westing ultimately was a good man wanting to improve the lives of those who he felt he had wronged. The money was the incentive but the hope was that each of them would unlock the potential in themselves that was there all along, which was, in the long run, Sam Westing's chess plan all along.

The Westing Game Symbols, Allegory and Motifs

Chess (Motif)

The game of chess is a consistent motif in *The Westing Game*. Chess is a game that requires forward thinking and planning, much like the actual game Sam Westing plotted. In order to play chess successfully, one has to always be one step ahead of one's opponent, and only the player best able to predict Sam Westing's game (Turtle) is able to succeed. She ends up teaching her niece chess, just like her uncle taught her.

The Bombs (Symbol)

The bombs are a symbol for the pent-up rage and unhappiness Angela feels at constantly being coddled and infantilized by her family and neighbors for her looks and her engagement to Denton. Her decision to take agency and put her own beauty in harm's way in order to feel more empowered explodes in her face, just like the bombs.

Turtle's Braid (Symbol)

Turtle is intelligent but is constantly made to feel that she takes a backseat to Angela in both her looks and the attention she gets from her mother. The braid she wears symbolizes a way for her to get attention, even if it's eventually negative (and she gives someone a good sharp kick in the shins). Eventually when the firework singes off her braid, it allows her to come into her own without her security blanket.

Diversity (Motif)

A motif of this novel lies in the diversity of its cast. Not only do we have Americans of different races like J.J. Ford and Mr. Hoo, we have recent immigrants to the country such as Mrs. Hoo, who each become more and more a part of the American fabric throughout the story. We also have diversity in age, from old Crow to young Turtle, and health, from disabled Chris and "wasting" Sydelle.

Seasons (Motif)

The seasons play a large motif in the novel and affect the mood and journey of the characters. Turtle first discovers old Sam Westing's body on a spooky Halloween evening, then the novel takes off in the fall. As the characters get paired up, the winter comes and the snow locks them inside together to get to know one another. Ultimately when spring comes, the mysteries have been solved and the tenants of Sunset Towers emerge as closer friends.

The Westing Game Metaphors and Similes

Gaping Like Statues (Simile)

The simile "gaping like statues" (Chapter 2) is used to describe Doug Hoo and Theo Theodorakis as they wait on the lawn for Turtle to emerge from the Westing mansion. This simile contrasts the usual activity of Doug and Theo with their stony, breathless stillness.

Standing Like a Dummy (Simile)

This simile is used in Chapter 8 to describe Angela as she watches Sydelle patronize Chris by saying, "he's got a smile that could break your heart." Angela at this point has not found her voice yet, and often says only what others want her to. She does not intervene, like a dummy.

Like a Turtle's (Simile)

Judge Ford notices Sam Westing's resemblance to a turtle for the first time as she gazes upon his photograph: "those piercing eyes, the Vandyke beard, that short beaked nose (like a turtle's)" (Chapter 22).

Played Us Like Puppets (Simile)

The ungrateful heirs all grumble after they believe that they have lost the Westing Game, claiming that Sam Westing cheated them, and played them "like puppets" (Chapter 27). In some ways, they are right; he predicted their moves. However, he treated them more like chess pieces, allowing them to exercise free will.

Stuck Up-Know-It-All-Marshmallow-Face-Doctor-Denton (Metaphor)

Turtle refers to her future brother-in-law with this metaphor in Chapter 3. Of course he doesn't have marshmallow for a face, but it really captures Denton's essence.

The Westing Game Irony

Sydelle Getting Attention

Sydelle schemes to get attention by pretending to have a rare wasting disease that will kill her in a matter of weeks. She paints crutches and speaks as loudly as possible about her disease to anyone that will listen. Interestingly enough, Sydelle becomes a major player in the Westing Game. Ironically, it is not her injury that gets her attention, but rather her skills as a secretary coming in handy. Sydelle is the only one who has the transcription of the will, making her a hot commodity within the Sunset Towers community.

Sydelle's Injury

The attention afforded to Sydelle comes to a head when after months of pretending to have the disease, she is ultimately injured by one of the bombs. She puts on a very brave face and in fact enjoys the attention of the doctors as she heals. Many people realize that her wasting disease is a sham, but it doesn't stop them from visiting her and buttering her up for clues to the Westing Game.

J.J. Ford's Debt

J.J. Ford still feels guilt at the money she was given by Sam Westing for her education and fears that he has returned to ask for the money back. She is so preoccupied with this fact that she gives the $10,000 left to her by Sam Westing in the will to her partner, Sandy McSouthers. When it is revealed that Sandy is in fact Sam Westing in disguise, she realizes that she has actually repaid the debt unintentionally. The situational irony of the transaction is only revealed after the "death" of Sandy.

Angela's Marriage to Denton

Angela was expected to be a housewife to Dr. Denton Deere and though she has reservations, she never spoke of them. Eventually, Angela takes the money she gets from the Westing Game and calls off her engagement to Denton to pursue a career as a doctor herself. Ironically, once she is a doctor, she finally has the self-confidence to marry her former fiancee as equals.

The Westing Game Imagery

Fourth of July

Sam Westing's flair for the dramatic is described in detail through his love for Fourth of July pageants and all things Fourth of July related. When the Westing mansion is ultimately destroyed, it goes out in a burst of red, white, and blue fireworks that celebrate Sam Westing's love of all things American.

Food

With two restaurants in Sunset Towers, there is quite a bit of food imagery in the novel. The description of the actual menu items at Shin Hoo's restaurant (the short ribs seems to be the specialty) and the items at the coffee shop are juxtaposed by the entrees made up by Sydelle and Chris, from "french fried mouse" to "chocolate covered moose."

Chess/Game

There are multiple mentions of chess and other competitions in the novel. Everyone begins to see themselves as a "pawn" in Sam Westing's chess game. At one point, when Crow is framed, J.J. Ford realizes that she is being sacrificed like the chess piece "the queen." In the backdrop, Doug Hoo's competitions and medals also inject the ideas of games, winners, and losers into the novel.

Paper Products

Sam Westing owns a paper factory and his products are scattered throughout the book. Westing Paper Products makes items such as disposable paper diapers (which he allegedly stole from Mr. Hoo). Mr. Hoo also has paper products of his own: his paper innersoles which he eventually sells and makes quite a bit of money.

The Westing Game The Westing Game Film Adaptation "Get A Clue" and Theatre Adaptation

In 1997, a made-for-TV adaptation of *The Westing Game* was release called "Get A Clue." It was written for the screen by Dylan Kelsey Hadley. It featured stage and screen actor Ray Walston as Sam Westing and child actress Ashley Peldon as Turtle Wexler. The adaptation streamlined much of the plot, removing characters such as Flora, Theo, Madame Hoo, and Denton. The film was met with mediocre reviews.

In 2008, Prime Stage Theatre in Pittsburgh commissioned an adaptation of *The Westing Game,* which kept its original title. It was adapted by Darian Lindle and directed by Terry Brino-Dean. Artistic director Wayne Brenda commissioned the novel to be adapted. The director had this to say about this adaptation: "The mystery is a game that's put together to accomplish another objective... It's more about bringing these people together to play a game than it is about the game itself."

The Westing Game Literary Elements

Genre

Mystery

Setting and Context

A Wisconsin town on Lake Michigan; the 1970s

Narrator and Point of View

The novel features a third-person omniscient narrator who has access to the actions and thoughts of the characters in the novel.

Tone and Mood

The tone is playful yet suspenseful, painting colorful characters in a bright light even against the somber backdrop of a murder mystery.

Protagonist and Antagonist

The protagonist is Turtle Wexler. The antagonist is originally thought to be the unknown murderer of Sam Westing, but truly there is no antagonist.

Major Conflict

The major conflicts are discovering who murdered Sam Westing and who will ultimately win his fortune.

Climax

The climax arrives when Turtle Wexler puts the inhabitants of Sunset Towers on trial and solves the mystery of the Westing Game.

Foreshadowing

The first chapter of the novel opens with a veiled piece of foreshadowing. When the narrator claims that Barney Northrup rented one apartment to the wrong person, he could be referring to Crow, who is truly Sam Westing's former wife, or Sydelle Pulaski, who was not connected to the Westings in any way. Sam Westing's cryptic will is also full of clues, including the cryptic warning that not everyone is who they claim to be.

Understatement

Sandy refers to the bombs as gas explosions when they are in fact intentionally placed bombs.

Allusions

The novel is full of allusions to classic Americana tropes, such as "America the Beautiful" and Uncle Sam. Everything Sam Westing does has an air of patriotism about it, hence why his will and clues are littered with so many allusions to patriotic icons.

Imagery

The novel is full of imagery related to weather as the seasons pass around Sunset Towers. Raskin goes to great lengths to paint the environment around Sunset Towers: the crisp October night on lake Michigan and the way Sunset Tower is snowed in for weeks. The author also goes to great detail describing personal attributes, such as the crutches of Sydelle Pulaski or the garb of Judge J.J. Ford.

Paradox

An example of paradox is when Sandy McSouthers is talking to Judge Ford about how poor his family is, when he is in fact Sam Westing in disguise and terribly rich.

Parallelism

There is a parallelism between the career of Sam Westing and T.R. Wexler; they both come from humble beginnings but through their drive and shrewdness ultimately become successful.

Metonymy and Synecdoche

N/A

Personification

N/A

The Westing Game Links

The Westing Game Essay Questions

1. **Describe how the pairs assigned by the Westing Game compliment each other. Give examples of how they improve each other's lives.**

   Sam Westing assigned the pairs by personalities and what each player needed to learn from the other. For example, Grace Wexler learns from Mr. Hoo's business savvy and grows to want to become more a part of his restaurant. Grace finding her own purpose also allows Angela to have space from her mother to grow. Sydelle grows in confidence through having Angela as a partner and this allows her to finally feel seen by her neighbors. Finally, Chris benefits from Denton's medical background and actually gets to experience treatment he would not have otherwise.

2. **Describe the dynamic in the Wexler family. Is it a happy one? Why or why not?**

   The Wexler family dynamic is not a happy one. Grace Wexler spends most of her time doting on Angela, making her feel forced into her upcoming marriage and largely ignoring Turtle. This attention on Angela makes Angela feel trapped into obeying the wishes of her mother rather than following her own path, which leads her to becoming the bomber. Dr. Wexler's finances are also an issue; he feels like a loser because he is not able to adequately support his family.

3. **How is the Westing Game a uniquely American novel?**

   The Westing Game celebrates the diversity of America and rewards uniquely American values. The inhabitants of Sunset Tower are from different ethnic backgrounds - Greek, Chinese, black, Polish, and Jewish - and different economic backgrounds - from very rich to very poor. Yet, they are all stronger when they are working together as a team and learn and grow from each other's cultures. Sam Westing's game also rewards hard work and gives people opportunities to improve themselves rather than simply giving them money. Ultimately those who work hard are rewarded and the *Westing Game* empowers the players to be their best selves.

4. **From Sam Westing's perspective, what is the point of the Westing Game?**

   For Sam Westing, his game is created as a form of penance for those who he feels he's wronged (his former wife) and a way to have fun and be generous to those who have played a role in his life. With Crow, he wants to give her the opportunity to move on and find happiness even without him, and the game allows him to bring her to their old home and give her money she would not accept from him directly. It also allows him to reward those who are a part of his life with a small amount of money to help them begin the search for what they truly want in life. After the Westing Game, Angela, who was simply going to be married, finds her passion and studies to become a doctor, largely because of the introspection that the game triggers in all of the players.

5. **Discuss J.J. Ford's journey with her own identity. What effect does the Westing Game have on it?**

Judge Ford is initially wracked with guilt over an unpaid loan the Sam Westing. We learn that he sponsored her to go to school and she never repaid the debt. She is sensitive about the fact that she received money from him, as well as the fact that her family acted as servants at his home. She is at first insulted by her clues "stars are shining brother" which she feels is a racial slight, but ultimately as she plays the game she grows more comfortable in her identity and finally pays back her debt directly to the man who gave her the money in the first place.

The Westing Game Quizzes

1. **What is the body of water Sunset Towers is on?**
    A. Lake Huron
    B. Lake Erie
    C. Lake Michigan
    D. Lake Ontario

2. **How many stories high is Sunset Towers?**
    A. 6
    B. 2
    C. 3
    D. 5

3. **Who were the first people to be shown Sunset Towers?**
    A. The Hoos
    B. Sydelle Pulaski
    C. Judge Ford
    D. The Wexlers

4. **We are warned that the tenants are all of the following EXCEPT?**
    A. A bookie
    B. A bomber
    C. A gardener
    D. A burglar

5. **What word best describes the atmosphere of Sunset Towers at the start of the book?**
    A. Cordial
    B. Angry
    C. Rude
    D. Close

6. **How many people came to Shin Hoo's Restaurant for the opening?**
    A. No one
    B. Three
    C. Fifty
    D. Hundreds

7. **Which of the following is the best example of imagery in the Westing Game?**
    A. Sports Gear
    B. Animals
    C. Weather
    D. Sunsets

8. **What appears at the Westing mansion that surprises the tenants?**
    A. Sad violin music
    B. Cars in the driveway
    C. Smoke from the chimney
    D. Dogs barking in the yard

9. **Why does Sandy McSouthers say he has a problem with Sam Westing?**
    A. He fired him from his factory.
    B. He stole money from him.
    C. He killed his dog.
    D. He stole his wife.

10. **What was Sam Westing's trade?**
    A. Fine dining
    B. Banking
    C. Academia
    D. Paper products

11. **Who is watching the group from inside Sunset Towers?**
    A. Shin Hoo
    B. Sydelle
    C. Chris
    D. Grace

12. **What does the person who dared to go inside the Westing House say sitting in the asylum over and over?**
    A. "Majesty"
    B. "Purple waves"
    C. "Westing's dead"
    D. "Not a game"

13. **Which of her children does Grace prefer?**
    A. Angela
    B. She dislikes both of them.
    C. She likes them both the same.
    D. Turtle

14. **What does Turtle do to those who pull her braid?**
    A. She tickles them.
    B. She punches them.
    C. She kicks their shin.
    D. She offers them a massage.

15. **Who is Dr. Wexler operating on during their talk about Sam Westing?**
   A. Shin Hoo
   B. Chris
   C. Crow
   D. Sydelle

16. **What concerns J.J. Ford about Sam Westing's return?**
   A. They were former lovers.
   B. She stole from him.
   C. They were business partners.
   D. She owes him money.

17. **What is Sydelle's biggest concern?**
   A. People are mean to her.
   B. No one notices her.
   C. Her singleness
   D. Her debt

18. **Which holiday does Turtle find the corpse on?**
   A. Easter
   B. Halloween
   C. Christmas
   D. President's Day

19. **What is the rate they agree to pay Turtle for every minute in the Westing mansion?**
   A. 10 dollars
   B. 2 dollars
   C. 50 cents
   D. 5 dollars

20. **What does Turtle hope to buy with this money?**
   A. A subscription to the Wall Street Journal
   B. A witch costume
   C. A new Mickey Mouse clock
   D. A puppy

21. **What does Sam Westing NOT say is a secret to his success?**
   A. Fair play
   B. Zest for life
   C. Clean living
   D. Hard work

22. **What does Sam Westing store in the basement of his home?**
   A. Guns
   B. Art
   C. Money
   D. Fireworks

23. **Who delivers the letters summoning the heirs?**
    A. E.J. Plum
    B. Otis Amber
    C. Sam Westing
    D. J.J. Ford

24. **How many heirs are there to Sam Westing's fortune?**
    A. 16
    B. 9
    C. 10
    D. 20

25. **What is NOT a position that Grace Wexler considers herself as?**
    A. Housewife
    B. A mother
    C. Heiress
    D. Decorator

Quiz 1 Answer Key

1. **(C)** Lake Michigan
2. **(D)** 5
3. **(D)** The Wexlers
4. **(C)** A gardener
5. **(A)** Cordial
6. **(B)** Three
7. **(C)** Weather
8. **(C)** Smoke from the chimney
9. **(A)** He fired him from his factory.
10. **(D)** Paper products
11. **(C)** Chris
12. **(B)** "Purple waves"
13. **(A)** Angela
14. **(C)** She kicks their shin.
15. **(C)** Crow
16. **(D)** She owes him money.
17. **(B)** No one notices her.
18. **(B)** Halloween
19. **(B)** 2 dollars
20. **(A)** A subscription to the Wall Street Journal
21. **(B)** Zest for life
22. **(D)** Fireworks
23. **(B)** Otis Amber
24. **(A)** 16
25. **(B)** A mother

The Westing Game Quizzes

1. **Which of the heirs truly believes he/she is related to Sam Westing?**
    A. Turtle
    B. Grace
    C. Jake
    D. Doug Hoo

2. **Which family from the building does not have all of its members as heirs?**
    A. The Hoo Family
    B. The Wexler Family
    C. All of the members of all families are heirs.
    D. The Theodorakis family

3. **Why does Doug tell off Flora?**
    A. She stuck him with a pin.
    B. She took up too many seats.
    C. She was late.
    D. She was talking to Chris like a baby.

4. **Who is E.J. Plum?**
    A. Westing's lawyer
    B. The murderer
    C. Westing's housekeeper
    D. Westing's doctor

5. **What about shaking Judge Ford's hand gives Grace Wexler pleasure?**
    A. It gives her the opportunity to get her to pardon her husband's gambling.
    B. She's black, so it makes her feel liberal.
    C. She was a former enemy, now friend.
    D. She's meeting such an important person.

6. **What does Sydelle pretend to have when she enters the Westing mansion?**
    A. A relation to Sam Westing
    B. A wasting disease
    C. A husband
    D. A new car

7. **How does Sam Westing refer to his heirs?**
    A. Nieces and nephews
    B. Girls and boys
    C. Lord and ladies
    D. Sons and daughters

8. **What does Sam Westing say happened to him?**
   A. He was buried.
   B. He was murdered.
   C. His life was taken.
   D. He was betrayed.

9. **How much money does each pair receive?**
   A. $1,000
   B. $100
   C. $10,000
   D. $500

10. **What are the clues?**
    A. Chess pieces
    B. Random words
    C. Photographs
    D. Maps

11. **Who took notes on the will?**
    A. Grace
    B. Sydelle
    C. Chris
    D. Angela

12. **Why does no one leave Sunset Towers the day after the will is read?**
    A. They are snowed in.
    B. The will told them not to go.
    C. They are scared to leave.
    D. They are hunting for clues.

13. **What does Sydelle say about Chris?**
    A. He is a traitor.
    B. He has no intolerance.
    C. He has a smile that could break your heart.
    D. He is the true heir.

14. **What does Turtle decide to do with her $10,000?**
    A. Hide it under her bed
    B. Put it in a savings account
    C. Put in in the stock market
    D. Donate it to charity

15. **What does Mr. Hoo hate most in Sunset Towers?**
    A. His restaurant
    B. The elevator
    C. The coffee shop
    D. The windows

16. **What game does Theo keep inviting tenants to play?**
    A. Tag
    B. Golf
    C. Scrabble
    D. Chess

17. **Who decides to throw the party for the tenants?**
    A. Mr. Hoo
    B. Judge Ford
    C. Theo
    D. Grace

18. **What idea did Sam Westing allegedly steal from Mr. Hoo?**
    A. The disposable paper diaper
    B. Spare rib recipes
    C. Paper clips
    D. Paper innersoles

19. **Who is the first to arrive at Judge Ford's party?**
    A. Turtle
    B. Chris and Theo
    C. Jake and Grace Wexler
    D. The Hoos

20. **Where does Mrs. Hoo want to go more than anything?**
    A. China
    B. The Westing mansion
    C. New York City
    D. Disney World

21. **What do Sydelle and Angela dress like for the party?**
    A. Uncle Sam
    B. Princesses
    C. Twins
    D. Elvis

22. **What does Mr. Hoo always say his son needs to do more of?**
    A. Eat
    B. Study
    C. Sleep
    D. Exercise

23. **Why does Angela cry at the party?**
    A. She has food poisoning.
    B. She doesn't feel anyone pays attention to her.
    C. She feels people only care about her engagement.
    D. Turtle kicked her.

24. **What is Judge Ford missing?**
   A. Her father's watch
   B. Her robes
   C. Her Mercedes
   D. Her law diploma

25. **Why can't the tenants read Sydelle's notes?**
   A. They're written in morse code.
   B. They were burned in a fire.
   C. She won't show them the notebook.
   D. They're written in Polish.

Quiz 2 Answer Key

1. **(B)** Grace
2. **(D)** The Theodorakis family
3. **(D)** She was talking to Chris like a baby.
4. **(A)** Westing's lawyer
5. **(B)** She's black, so it makes her feel liberal.
6. **(B)** A wasting disease
7. **(A)** Nieces and nephews
8. **(C)** His life was taken.
9. **(C)** $10,000
10. **(B)** Random words
11. **(B)** Sydelle
12. **(A)** They are snowed in.
13. **(C)** He has a smile that could break your heart.
14. **(C)** Put in in the stock market
15. **(C)** The coffee shop
16. **(D)** Chess
17. **(B)** Judge Ford
18. **(A)** The disposable paper diaper
19. **(C)** Jake and Grace Wexler
20. **(A)** China
21. **(C)** Twins
22. **(B)** Study
23. **(C)** She feels people only care about her engagement.
24. **(A)** Her father's watch
25. **(D)** They're written in Polish.

The Westing Game Quizzes

1. **What is Turtle's real name?**
   A. Tabitha-Ruth
   B. Alice
   C. Carol
   D. Hillary

2. **Where does the first bomb go off?**
   A. The coffee shop
   B. The Westing mansion
   C. Mr. Hoo's restaurant
   D. Judge Ford's apartment

3. **What does Angela think Turtle's "crutch" is?**
   A. Her newspapers
   B. Her Mickey Mouse clock
   C. Her shin-kicking
   D. Her braid

4. **Who does Sydelle eat with at Hoo's restaurant before the bomb goes off?**
   A. Jake
   B. Chris
   C. Denton
   D. Flora

5. **What does Sydelle find interesting about sitting with the person she's with?**
   A. They're both Polish.
   B. They're both married.
   C. They're both women.
   D. They're both disabled.

6. **Why doesn't Theo go to college?**
   A. He doesn't have good grades.
   B. The money is going to Chris's operation.
   C. He doesn't know what he wants to do.
   D. He didn't get in.

7. **Who else did Flora make a wedding dress for besides Angela?**
   A. J.J. Ford
   B. Violet Westing
   C. Catherine Theodorakis
   D. Grace Wexler

8. **What is the only way to solve the clues from the will?**
   A. Put them under a blacklight
   B. Put all of the pairs' clues together
   C. Unscramble the letters
   D. Turn them upside down

9. **Why doesn't Chris sign his check so Denton can deposit it?**
   A. He can't sign it physically.
   B. He doesn't have a bank account.
   C. He wants the money for himself.
   D. He wants Denton to keep coming back.

10. **What does Grace want to rename Shin Hoo's Restaurant?**
    A. Hoo's on First
    B. Hoo's Dumplings
    C. Panda Express
    D. Wexler's Eats

11. **Why does Sandy say he can't play chess with Theo?**
    A. He has a wasting disease.
    B. He doesn't know the game.
    C. He would rather play Hearts.
    D. He doesn't want to lose.

12. **Why did Violet Westing allegedly kill herself?**
    A. She was being forced to marry a crooked state senator.
    B. She was in love with a man who died.
    C. She was diagnosed with cancer.
    D. She had gambling debts.

13. **Where does the third bomb go off?**
    A. The Westing mansion
    B. J.J. Ford's apartment
    C. The parking lot
    D. Angela's bridal shower

14. **What gift does Angela get two of?**
    A. An asparagus cooker
    B. An egg poacher
    C. A television set
    D. A radio

15. **What does the third bomb cause to happen in Sunset Towers?**
    A. Paranoia
    B. The demolition of the building
    C. Isolation
    D. Eviction

16. **What does Turtle decide to call Mrs. Baumbach?**
    A. Baba
    B. Big Sister
    C. Daddy
    D. Lady

17. **Who claims to have given Mr. Hoo the idea for paper innersoles?**
    A. Judge Ford
    B. Otis
    C. Crow
    D. Sandy

18. **What is Turtle's newspaper of choice?**
    A. The New York Times
    B. The Madison Herald
    C. The Chicago Tribune
    D. The Wall Street Journal

19. **Who is the chairman of the Westing Paper Products company?**
    A. Bethany Feller
    B. Tom Jacksonville
    C. Harry North
    D. Julian Eastman

20. **What does Flora do that makes Turtle jealous?**
    A. Talk about her daughter Rosalie
    B. Tell Turtle she wishes she had Doug Hoo as a son
    C. Make a dress for Angela
    D. Hug Angela

21. **How did Rosalie die?**
    A. Drowning
    B. Pneumonia
    C. Suicide
    D. A car accident

22. **What does Theo ask of Doug Hoo?**
    A. To chase Turtle
    B. To follow Otis Amber
    C. To go to the Westing mansion
    D. To learn chess

23. **What does Denton do for Chris?**
    A. He gives him an internship.
    B. He gives him medicine to help with his condition.
    C. He gives him all the money.
    D. He donates a kidney.

24. **What is Sam Westing's real name?**
       A. Windy Windkloppel
       B. Olly Nosegay
       C. Peter Frampton
       D. Sal Westingbird

25. **Was Turtle's endeavor to invest her money a smart one?**
       A. Yes, they made a profit.
       B. Yes, even though they lost money they learned.
       C. No, they lost money.
       D. No, they made money but it caused tension with Flora.

Quiz 3 Answer Key

1. **(A)** Tabitha-Ruth
2. **(A)** The coffee shop
3. **(D)** Her braid
4. **(B)** Chris
5. **(D)** They're both disabled.
6. **(B)** The money is going to Chris's operation.
7. **(B)** Violet Westing
8. **(B)** Put all of the pairs' clues together
9. **(D)** He wants Denton to keep coming back.
10. **(A)** Hoo's on First
11. **(B)** He doesn't know the game.
12. **(A)** She was being forced to marry a crooked state senator.
13. **(D)** Angela's bridal shower
14. **(A)** An asparagus cooker
15. **(A)** Paranoia
16. **(A)** Baba
17. **(D)** Sandy
18. **(D)** The Wall Street Journal
19. **(D)** Julian Eastman
20. **(A)** Talk about her daughter Rosalie
21. **(B)** Pneumonia
22. **(B)** To follow Otis Amber
23. **(B)** He gives him medicine to help with his condition.
24. **(A)** Windy Windkloppel
25. **(A)** Yes, they made a profit.

The Westing Game Quizzes

1. **Which member of the Westing family does J.J. Ford realize must be one of the heirs?**
   A. Sam Westing
   B. Mrs. Westing
   C. Greg Westing
   D. Violet Westing

2. **Where does Crow go in the city so often?**
   A. The Krazy Kids Skating Rink
   B. The Polka Dot Diner
   C. The Wesley Willows Old Folks Home
   D. The Good Salvation Soup Kitchen

3. **What is J.J. Ford's connection to the Westings?**
   A. She was his lawyer.
   B. She was his daughter's best friend.
   C. She was the daughter of his servants.
   D. She was his girlfriend.

4. **Why is J.J. Ford indebted to Sam Westing?**
   A. He adopted her.
   B. He bailed her out of jail.
   C. He saved her life.
   D. He paid for her education.

5. **How does the third bomb hurt Turtle?**
   A. It burns off her braid.
   B. It hits her in the stomach.
   C. It blows off her arms.
   D. It cuts her cheek.

6. **Who questions Turtle about the bomb?**
   A. Sandy
   B. Flora
   C. Judge Ford
   D. Angela

7. **Why does Turtle ask for Bourbon?**
   A. To sell it
   B. To ease the pain in her cavity
   C. To give to Angela
   D. To sleep

8. **Who is the thief of the possessions of Sunset Towers?**
   A. Mrs. Hoo
   B. Theo
   C. Crow
   D. Sandy

9. **Why does he/she steal?**
   A. To pay for college
   B. To disguise himself
   C. To save money to go back to China
   D. To buy food for the soup kitchen

10. **Who is the former Mrs. Westing?**
    A. Mrs. Hoo
    B. Grace
    C. Flora
    D. Crow

11. **Why does Chris think Sam Westing must be a good man?**
    A. He built Sunset Towers.
    B. He gave everyone the perfect partner to make friends.
    C. He owns the soup kitchen.
    D. He gave them all a lot more money the second time.

12. **What do the clues spell out?**
    A. A Shakespeare sonnet
    B. The lyrics to "America the Beautiful"
    C. The Declaration of Independence
    D. All of the letters of Otis Amber's birth certificate

13. **What name is missing from the clues?**
    A. Berthe Erica Crow
    B. Otis Amber
    C. Turtle Wexler
    D. Sandy McSouthers

14. **Who reveals themselves as the person who is the answer?**
    A. Mr. Hoo
    B. Crow
    C. Otis Amber
    D. Flora

15. **What does Turtle do to Barney Northrup when he comes to scold her family?**
    A. She apologizes.
    B. She takes off his disguise.
    C. She kicks him in the shins.
    D. She punches him in the face.

16. **What is Sam Westing's real last name?**
     A. Northrup
     B. Crow
     C. Hoo
     D. Windkloppel

17. **What is Otis Amber's true occupation?**
     A. A private investigator
     B. A gardener
     C. A doctor
     D. A lawyer

18. **What is ironic about Judge Ford giving the $10,000 to Sandy?**
     A. The check will bounce.
     B. She is really paying the murderer.
     C. She is unknowingly paying off the debt for her education.
     D. He stole that much money from her.

19. **Which is not one of Sam Westing's identities?**
     A. Bette Mapston
     B. Barney Northrup
     C. Julian Eastman
     D. Sandy McSouthers

20. **What is Sam Westing's final gift to the tenants of Sunset Towers?**
     A. A pile of gold
     B. The Westing mansion
     C. More money
     D. The deed to the building

21. **What happens to the Westing house?**
     A. It burns down as the fireworks go off.
     B. It is sold to Angela and Denton.
     C. It is destroyed in a hurricane.
     D. It is given to the tenants of Sunset Towers.

22. **What does Angela do before she marries Denton?**
     A. She becomes a doctor.
     B. Nothing, they get married immediately.
     C. She changes her name to Violet.
     D. She moves to New York.

23. **Who has their wedding in Sunset Tower?**
     A. Sydelle and Chris
     B. Otis Amber and Crow
     C. Denton and Angela
     D. Jake and Grace, renewing their vows

24. **How does Turtle win the Westing game?**
      A. She finds the money buried in the rubble of the Westing house.
      B. She finds Julian Eastman.
      C. She wins a game of chess against Judge Ford.
      D. She makes the most money at the stock market.

25. **What game does Turtle teach her niece in the epilogue?**
      A. Chess
      B. Checkers
      C. Sorry
      D. Dominos

Quiz 4 Answer Key

1. **(B)** Mrs. Westing
2. **(D)** The Good Salvation Soup Kitchen
3. **(C)** She was the daughter of his servants.
4. **(D)** He paid for her education.
5. **(A)** It burns off her braid.
6. **(C)** Judge Ford
7. **(B)** To ease the pain in her cavity
8. **(A)** Mrs. Hoo
9. **(C)** To save money to go back to China
10. **(D)** Crow
11. **(B)** He gave everyone the perfect partner to make friends.
12. **(B)** The lyrics to "America the Beautiful"
13. **(A)** Berthe Erica Crow
14. **(B)** Crow
15. **(C)** She kicks him in the shins.
16. **(D)** Windkloppel
17. **(A)** A private investigator
18. **(C)** She is unknowingly paying off the debt for her education.
19. **(A)** Bette Mapston
20. **(D)** The deed to the building
21. **(A)** It burns down as the fireworks go off.
22. **(A)** She becomes a doctor.
23. **(B)** Otis Amber and Crow
24. **(B)** She finds Julian Eastman.
25. **(A)** Chess

The Westing Game Bibliography

Hintz, Martin . Wisconsin Off the Beaten Path: A Guide To Unique Places . New York: Globe Pequot Press, 2012.

Sherr, Lynn . America the Beautiful: The Stirring True Story Behind Our Nation's Favorite Song. New York: PublicAffairs, 2001.

Beinhart, Larry . How to Write a Mystery . New York: Ballantine Book, 1996 .

Prime Stage Theatre. "2008-2009 Season: The Westing Game." Sept 20, 2017. <http://www.primestage.com/shows_and_tickets/archives_twg.html>.

"The Westing Game (1997)." Sept 20, 2017. <http://www.imdb.com/title/tt0120495/?ref_=nm_flmg_act_126>.

Gormly, Kelly B. . ""Westing Game" Makes World Debut at Hazlett." Wednesday, April 29, 2009. Sept 20, 2017. <http://triblive.com/x/pittsburghtrib/ae/theater/s_622892.html>.

ClassicNotes

GradeSaver™

Getting you the grade since 1999™

Other ClassicNotes from GradeSaver™

12 Angry Men	A Journal of the	Americanah
1984	Plague Year	American Beauty
8 1/2	Alas, Babylon	A Midsummer
Absalom, Absalom	A Lesson Before	Night's Dream
A Burnt-Out Case	Dying	A Modest Proposal
Accidental Death of	Alice in Wonderland	and Other Satires
an Anarchist	Alien	Amusing Ourselves
A Child Called "It"	All Creatures Great	to Death
A Christmas Carol	and Small	Anatomy of
A Clockwork	Allegiant	Criticism
Orange	Allen Ginsberg's	Andrew Marvell:
A Clockwork	Poetry	Poems
Orange (Film)	All My Sons	And Then There
A Confederacy of	All Quiet on the	Were None
Dunces	Western Front	An Enemy of the
Adam Bede	All the King's Men	People
A Doll's House	All the Light We	Angela's Ashes
A Farewell to Arms	Cannot See	An Ideal Husband
Agamemnon	All the Pretty Horses	Animal Farm
A Grain of Wheat	A Long Way Gone	An Inspector Calls
A Grave	A Lost Lady	Anna Karenina
A Hero of Our Time	Altered	Anne Bradstreet:
A Hunger Artist	Amadeus	Poems

For our full list of over 250 Study Guides, Quizzes,
Sample College Application Essays, Literature Essays and E-texts, visit:

www.gradesaver.com

ClassicNotes

GradeSaver™

Getting you the grade since 1999™

Other ClassicNotes from GradeSaver™

Anthem
Antigone
Antony and
  Cleopatra
A&P and Other
  Stories
A Passage to India
Apocalypse Now
A Psalm of Life
A Raisin in the Sun
Arcadia
Are You There God?
  It's Me, Margaret.
Aristotle:
  Nicomachean
  Ethics
Aristotle's Poetics
Aristotle's Politics
Arms and the Man
A Room of One's
  Own
A Room With a
  View

A Rose For Emily
  and Other Short
  Stories
Around the World in
  80 Days
A Sentimental
  Journey Through
  France and Italy
A Separate Peace
As I Lay Dying
A Streetcar Named
  Desire
Astrophil and Stella
A Study in Scarlet
As You Like It
A Tale of Two Cities
A Thousand
  Splendid Suns
Atlantia
Atlas Shrugged
Atonement

A Very Old Man
  With Enormous
  Wings
A View From the
  Bridge
A Vindication of the
  Rights of Woman
A White Heron and
  Other Stories
A Wrinkle in Time
Babbitt
Balzac and the Little
  Chinese
  Seamstress
Bartleby the
  Scrivener
Bastard Out of
  Carolina
Beloved
Benito Cereno
Beowulf
Between the World
  and Me

For our full list of over 250 Study Guides, Quizzes,
Sample College Application Essays, Literature Essays and E-texts, visit:

www.gradesaver.com

ClassicNotes

GrAdeSaver™

Getting you the grade since 1999™

Other ClassicNotes from GradeSaver™

Bhagavad-Gita
Billy Budd
Black Beauty
Black Boy
Black Skin, White
  Masks
Blade Runner
Bleak House
Bless Me, Ultima
Blindness
Blink
Blood Meridian: Or
  the Evening
  Redness in the
  West
Blood Wedding
Bluest Eye
Brave New World
Breakfast at
  Tiffany's
Breakfast of
  Champions
Burmese Days

By Night in Chile
Call of the Wild
Candide
Cane
Cannery Row
Casablanca
Catch-22
Catching Fire
Cathedral
Cat on a Hot Tin
  Roof
Cat's Cradle
Ceremony
Charlie and the
  Chocolate Factory
Charlotte's Web
Charlotte Temple
Childhood's End
Children of Men
Chinese Cinderella
Christina Rossetti:
  Poems
Christmas Bells

Christopher
  Marlowe's Poems
Chronicle of a Death
  Foretold
Citizen: An
  American Lyric
Citizen Kane
Civil Disobedience
Civilization and Its
  Discontents
Civil Peace
Cloud Atlas
Clueless
Coleridge's Poems
Comedy of Errors
Communist
  Manifesto
Confessions
Confessions of an
  English Opium
  Eater

For our full list of over 250 Study Guides, Quizzes,
Sample College Application Essays, Literature Essays and E-texts, visit:

www.gradesaver.com

Other ClassicNotes from GradeSaver™

Connecticut Yankee in King Arthur's Court
Coriolanus
Crewel
Crime and Punishment
Crossed
Cry, the Beloved Country
Cymbeline
Cyrano de Bergerac
Daisy Miller
David Copperfield
Dead Poets Society
Death and the King's Horseman
Death and the Maiden
Death in Venice
Death of a Salesman
Democracy in America

Desiree's Baby
Desire Under the Elms
Devil in a Blue Dress
Dharma Bums
Disgrace
Divergent
Divine Comedy-I: Inferno
Do Androids Dream of Electric Sheep?
Doctor Faustus (Marlowe)
Dombey and Son
Don Quixote Book I
Don Quixote Book II
Dora: An Analysis of a Case of Hysteria
Dracula

Dr. Jekyll and Mr. Hyde
Dr. Strangelove
Dubliners
East of Eden
Edgar Huntly: Memoirs of a Sleep-Walker
Educating Rita
El Despertar
Electra by Sophocles
Emily Dickinson's Collected Poems
Emma
Ender's Game
Endgame
Enduring Love
Enrique's Journey
Equus
Esperanza Rising
Eternal Sunshine of the Spotless Mind

ClassicNotes

GrﾑdeSaver™

Getting you the grade since 1999™

Other ClassicNotes from GradeSaver™

Ethan Frome
Eugene Onegin
Evangeline; A Tale
   of Acadie
Evelina
Everyday Use
Everyman: Morality
   Play
Everything is
   Illuminated
Exeter Book
Extremely Loud and
   Incredibly Close
Ezra Pound: Poems
Facundo: Or,
   Civilization and
   Barbarism
Fahrenheit 451
Fallen Angels
Fantastic Mr. Fox
Fantomina
Fear and Loathing in
   Las Vegas

Fences
Fifth Business
Fight Club
Fight Club (Film)
Flags of Our Fathers
Flannery O'Connor's
   Stories
Flight
Flowers for
   Algernon
Foe
For Colored Girls
   Who Have
   Considered
   Suicide When the
   Rainbow Is Enuf
For Whom the Bell
   Tolls
Founding Brothers
Frankenstein
Franny and Zooey
Freakonomics
Friday Night Lights

From the Mixed-Up
   Files of Mrs.
   Basil E.
   Frankweiler
Fun Home
Gargantua and
   Pantagruel
Gattaca
Gilead
Girl With a Pearl
   Earring
Goethe's Faust
Gone Girl
Gorilla, My Love
Go Set a Watchman
Go Tell it On the
   Mountain
Great Expectations
Green Grass,
   Running Water
Grendel
Gulliver's Travels
Hamlet

For our full list of over 250 Study Guides, Quizzes,
Sample College Application Essays, Literature Essays and E-texts, visit:

www.gradesaver.com

ClassicNotes

GrAdeSaver™

Getting you the grade since 1999™

Other ClassicNotes from GradeSaver™

Hard Times

Haroun and the Sea of Stories

Harriet the Spy

Harry Potter and the Cursed Child

Harry Potter and the Philosopher's Stone

Hatchet

Heart of Darkness

Hedda Gabler

Henry IV Part 1

Henry IV Part 2

Henry IV (Pirandello)

Henry V

Herzog

Hippolytus

Hiroshima

Holes

Homegoing

Homo Faber

House of Mirth

House on Mango Street

Howards End

How the Garcia Girls Lost Their Accents

How to Read Literature Like a Professor

I Am Malala

I, Claudius

I for Isobel

I Know Why the Caged Bird Sings

Iliad

Incidents in the Life of a Slave Girl

In Cold Blood

Inherit the Wind

In Our Time

Insurgent

Interpreter of Maladies

In the Heart of the Sea: The Tragedy of the Whaleship Essex

In the Penal Colony

In the Skin of a Lion

In the Time of the Butterflies

Into the Wild

Into Thin Air

Invisible Man

Ishmael

Island of the Blue Dolphins

It's Kind of a Funny Story

I Will Marry When I Want

James and the Giant Peach

Jane Eyre

For our full list of over 250 Study Guides, Quizzes,
Sample College Application Essays, Literature Essays and E-texts, visit:

www.gradesaver.com

ClassicNotes

GradeSaver™

Getting you the grade since 1999™

Other ClassicNotes from GradeSaver™

Lolita
Long Day's Journey
   Into Night
Look Back in Anger
Looking for Alaska
Lord Byron's Poems
Lord Jim
Lord of the Flies
Love in the Time of
   Cholera
Love Medicine
Lucy
Lying Awake
Macbeth
Mac Flecknoe
Madame Bovary
Maestro
Maggie: A Girl of
   the Streets and
   Other Stories
Manhattan Transfer
Maniac Magee

Mankind: Medieval
   Morality Plays
Mansfield Park
Mapping the
   Margins:
   Intersectionality,
   Identity Politics,
   and Violence
   against Women of
   Color
Marriage (Poem)
Mary Barton
Master Harold...
   And the Boys
Matched
Matilda
Matthew Arnold:
   Poems
MAUS
Measure for
   Measure
Medea
Merchant of Venice

Metamorphoses
Midaq Alley
Middlemarch
Middlesex
Midnight's Children
Miss Peregrine's
   Home for Peculiar
   Children
Moby Dick
Mockingjay
Moll Flanders
Monkey: A Folk
   Novel of China
Moonlight (Film)
Mother Courage and
   Her Children
Mrs. Dalloway
Mrs. Warren's
   Profession
Much Ado About
   Nothing
Murder in the
   Cathedral

For our full list of over 250 Study Guides, Quizzes,
Sample College Application Essays, Literature Essays and E-texts, visit:

www.gradesaver.com

ClassicNotes

GradeSaver™

Getting you the grade since 1999™

Other ClassicNotes from GradeSaver™

My Antonia
My Brilliant Friend
My Children! My
    Africa!
Mythology
Narrative of the Life
    of Frederick
    Douglass
Native Son
Nervous Conditions
Never Let Me Go
New Introductory
    Lectures on
    Psychoanalysis
News from Nowhere
Nickel and Dimed:
    On (Not) Getting
    By in America
Night
Nine Stories
Njal's Saga
No Exit
No Longer at Ease

North and South
Northanger Abbey
North by Northwest
Norwegian Wood
Notes from
    Underground
Number the Stars
Oedipus Rex or
    Oedipus the King
Of Mice and Men
Of Modern Poetry
Oliver Twist
On Beauty
One Day in the Life
    of Ivan
    Denisovich
One Flew Over the
    Cuckoo's Nest
One Flew Over the
    Cuckoo's Nest
    (Film)
One Hundred Years
    of Solitude

On Liberty
On the Road
On the Waterfront
O Pioneers
Oroonoko
Oryx and Crake
Othello
Our Town
Outcasts United
Outliers
Pale Fire
Pamela: Or Virtue
    Rewarded
Paper Towns
Parable of the Sower
Paradise
Paradise Lost
Passing
Paul Revere's Ride
Peace Like a River
Pedro Paramo
Percy Shelley:
    Poems

For our full list of over 250 Study Guides, Quizzes,
Sample College Application Essays, Literature Essays and E-texts, visit:

www.gradesaver.com

ClassicNotes

GradeSaver™

Getting you the grade since 1999™

Other ClassicNotes from GradeSaver™

Perfume: The Story of a Murderer
Persepolis: The Story of a Childhood
Persuasion
Phaedra
Phaedrus
Pilgrim's Progress
Poems of W.B. Yeats: The Rose
Poems of W.B. Yeats: The Tower
Poe's Poetry
Poe's Short Stories
Poetry
Politics and the English Language
Pope's Poems and Prose
Portrait of the Artist as a Young Man
Pretty Woman

Pride and Prejudice
Private Memoirs and Confessions of a Justified Sinner
Prometheus Bound
Psycho
Pudd'nhead Wilson
Purple Hibiscus
Pygmalion
Rabbit, Run
Rashomon
Ray Bradbury: Short Stories
Reached
Reading Lolita in Tehran
Rear Window
Rebecca
Reflections on Gandhi
Regeneration
Return of the Native
Rhinoceros

Richard II
Richard III
Riders to the Sea
Rip Van Winkle and Other Stories
Robert Browning: Poems
Robert Frost: Poems
Robinson Crusoe
Roll of Thunder, Hear My Cry
Roman Fever and Other Stories
Romeo and Juliet
Romeo and Juliet (Film 1968)
Roots
Rope
Rosencrantz and Guildenstern Are Dead
Rudyard Kipling: Poems

For our full list of over 250 Study Guides, Quizzes,
Sample College Application Essays, Literature Essays and E-texts, visit:

www.gradesaver.com

ClassicNotes

GradeSaver™

Getting you the grade since 1999™

Other ClassicNotes from GradeSaver™

Salome

Salvage the Bones

Schindler's List

Season of Migration
to the North

Second Treatise of
Government

Secret Sharer

Self Reliance and
Other Essays

Sense and
Sensibility

Shakespeare's
Sonnets

Shantaram

She Stoops to
Conquer

Shooting an
Elephant

Short Stories of
Ernest
Hemingway

Short Stories of F.
Scott Fitzgerald

Siddhartha

Silas Marner

Silence

Sir Gawain and the
Green Knight

Sir Thomas Wyatt:
Poems

Sister Carrie

Six Characters in
Search of an
Author

Slaughterhouse Five

Snow Country

Snow Falling on
Cedars

Something Wicked
This Way Comes

Song of Roland

Song of Solomon

Songs of Innocence
and of Experience

Sonny's Blues

Sons and Lovers

Speak

Spenser's Amoretti
and Epithalamion

Spring Awakening

Station Eleven

Sula

Sundiata: An Epic of
Old Mali

Sweat

Sylvia Plath: Poems

Symposium by Plato

Tamburlaine the
Great

Tangerine

Tartuffe

Taxi Driver

Tell Me a Riddle

Tender is the Night

Tennyson's Poems

Tess of the
D'Urbervilles

For our full list of over 250 Study Guides, Quizzes,
Sample College Application Essays, Literature Essays and E-texts, visit:

www.gradesaver.com

ClassicNotes

Gr**A**deSaver™

Getting you the grade since 1999™

Other ClassicNotes from GradeSaver™

That Was Then, This
 is Now
The 5th Wave
The Absolutely True
 Diary of a Part-
 Time Indian
The Adventures of
 Augie March
The Adventures of
 Huckleberry Finn
The Adventures of
 Tom Sawyer
The Aeneid
The Age of
 Innocence
The Alchemist
 (Coelho)
The Alchemist
 (Jonson)
The Ambassadors
The American
The Analects of
 Confucius

The Arabian Nights:
 One Thousand
 and One Nights
The Autobiography
 of an Ex-Colored
 Man
The Autobiography
 of Benjamin
 Franklin
The Awakening
The Bacchae
The Bean Trees
The Beggar's Opera
The Bell Jar
The Bet
The BFG
The Big Sleep (1946
 Film)
The Birthday Party
The Blithedale
 Romance
The Bloody
 Chamber

The Bonfire of the
 Vanities
The Book of Daniel
The Book of the
 Duchess and
 Other Poems
The Book Thief
The Boy in the
 Striped Pajamas
The Brief Wondrous
 Life of Oscar Wao
The Brothers
 Karamazov
The Burning Plain
 and Other Stories
The Canterbury
 Tales
The Caretaker
The Castle of
 Otranto
The Catcher in the
 Rye

For our full list of over 250 Study Guides, Quizzes,
Sample College Application Essays, Literature Essays and E-texts, visit:

www.gradesaver.com

ClassicNotes

GradeSaver™

Getting you the grade since 1999™

Other ClassicNotes from GradeSaver™

The Caucasian Chalk Circle

The Cherry Orchard

The Children's Hour

The Chocolate War

The Chosen

The Chrysalids

The Chrysanthemums

The Circle

The Clash of Civilizations

The Collector

The Color of Water

The Color Purple

The Consolation of Philosophy

The Conversation

The Coquette

The Count of Monte Cristo

The Country of the Pointed Firs and Other Stories

The Country Wife

The Cricket in Times Square

The Crucible

The Crying of Lot 49

The Curious Incident of the Dog in the Night-time

The Day Is Done

The Death Cure

The Death of Ivan Ilych

The Devil and Tom Walker

The Devil's Arithmetic

The Diary of a Young Girl by Anne Frank

The Drover's Wife

The Duchess of Malfi

The Dumb Waiter

The Electric Kool-Aid Acid Test

The Emperor of Ice Cream

The English Patient

The Epic of Gilgamesh

The Eumenides

The Faerie Queene

The Fall of the House of Usher

The Fault in Our Stars

The Federalist Papers

The Fish

For our full list of over 250 Study Guides, Quizzes, Sample College Application Essays, Literature Essays and E-texts, visit:

www.gradesaver.com

ClassicNotes

GrⱭdeSaver™

Getting you the grade since 1999™

Other ClassicNotes from GradeSaver™

The Jew of Malta

The Joy Luck Club

The Jungle

The Kill Order

The Kite Runner

The Lais of Marie
de France

The Legend of
Sleepy Hollow

The Library of
Babel

The Life of Olaudah
Equiano

The Lightning Thief

The Lion and the
Jewel

The Lion, the Witch
and the Wardrobe

The Lone Ranger
and Tonto
Fistfight in
Heaven

The Lord of the
Rings: The
Fellowship of the
Ring

The Lord of the
Rings: The Return
of the King

The Lord of the
Rings: The Two
Towers

The Lottery and
Other Stories

The Lovely Bones

The Love Song of J.
Alfred Prufrock

The Magician's
Nephew

The Maltese Falcon
(1941 Film)

The Man in the High
Castle

The Man of Mode

The Marrow of
Tradition

The Master and
Margarita

The Mayor of
Casterbridge

The Maze Runner

The Metamorphosis

The Mill on the
Floss

The Monk

The Monkey's Paw

The Moonlit Road
and Other Ghost
and Horror
Stories

The Moonstone

The Most
Dangerous Game

The Murder of
Roger Ackroyd

The Namesake

For our full list of over 250 Study Guides, Quizzes,
Sample College Application Essays, Literature Essays and E-texts, visit:

www.gradesaver.com

ClassicNotes

GradeSaver™

Getting you the grade since 1999™

Other ClassicNotes from GradeSaver™

The Narrative of
Arthur Gordon
Pym of Nantucket
The Necklace
The New Jim Crow
The Odyssey
The Old Man and
the Sea
The Once and
Future King
The Open Window
The Origin of
Species
The Origins of
Totalitarianism
The Outcasts of
Poker Flat
The Outsiders
The Outsiders (film)
The Overcoat
The Pact
The Painted Veil
The Paper Nautilus

The Pearl
The Perks of Being
a Wallflower
The Phantom of the
Opera
The Phantom
Tollbooth
The Piano Lesson
The Picture of
Dorian Gray
The Playboy of the
Western World
The Poems of
William Blake
The Poisonwood
Bible
The Portrait of a
Lady
The Praise of Folly
The Prince
The Princess Bride
(film)

The Professor's
House
The Protestant Ethic
and the Spirit of
Capitalism
The Quiet American
The Ramayana
The Real Inspector
Hound
The Real Life of
Sebastian Knight
The Red Badge of
Courage
The Remains of the
Day
The Republic
Therese Raquin
The Revenger's
Tragedy
The Rime of the
Ancient Mariner
The Road

For our full list of over 250 Study Guides, Quizzes,
Sample College Application Essays, Literature Essays and E-texts, visit:

www.gradesaver.com

ClassicNotes

GrAdeSaver™

Getting you the grade since 1999™

Other ClassicNotes from GradeSaver™

The Vicar of
Wakefield
The Visit
The Wars
The Waste Land
The Watsons Go to
Birmingham -
1963
The Wave
The Way of the
World
The Wealth of
Nations
The Westing Game
The Whale Rider
The White Devil
The White Tiger
The Wind in the
Willows
The Winter's Tale
The Witches
The Woman in
White

The Woman Warrior
The Wonderful
Wizard of Oz
The Wretched of the
Earth
The Yellow
Wallpaper
The Young Elites
The Zoo Story
Things Fall Apart
Thinking Sex
Thirteen Reasons
Why
Thirteen Ways of
Looking at a
Blackbird
Three Cups of Tea
Three Day Road
Three Men in a Boat
(To Say Nothing
of the Dog)
Through the
Looking Glass

Thus Spoke
Zarathustra
Titus Andronicus
Tobermory
To Build a Fire
To Kill a
Mockingbird
Top Girls
To the Lighthouse
Touching Spirit Bear
Treasure Island
Trifles
Troilus and Cressida
Tropic of Cancer
Tropic of Capricorn
Tuesdays With
Morrie
Twelfth Night
Twilight
Ulysses
Uncle Tom's Cabin
Under the Feet of
Jesus

For our full list of over 250 Study Guides, Quizzes,
Sample College Application Essays, Literature Essays and E-texts, visit:

www.gradesaver.com

ClassicNotes

GradeSaver™

Getting you the grade since 1999™

Other ClassicNotes from GradeSaver™

Untouchable
Up From Slavery
Ursula Le Guin:
  Short Stories
Utilitarianism
Utopia
Vanity Fair
Vanka
Villette
Volpone
Waiting for Godot
Waiting for Lefty
Waiting for the
  Barbarians
Walden
Walled States,
  Waning
  Sovereignty
Walt Whitman:
  Poems

War and Peace
Washington Square
We
Weep Not, Child
We Need New
  Names
What is the What
W. H. Auden:
  Poems
Where Are You
  Going, Where
  Have You Been?
Where the Red Fern
  Grows
White Fang
White Noise
White Teeth
Who's Afraid of
  Virginia Woolf
Wide Sargasso Sea

Wieland
Wilfred Owen:
  Poems
Winesburg, Ohio
Wise Blood
Women in Love
Wonder
Wordsworth's
  Poetical Works
Woyzeck
Wuthering Heights
Year of Wonders
Yonnondio: From
  the Thirties
Young Goodman
  Brown and Other
  Hawthorne Short
  Stories
Zeitoun
Z For Zachariah

For our full list of over 250 Study Guides, Quizzes,
Sample College Application Essays, Literature Essays and E-texts, visit:

www.gradesaver.com

Made in United States
North Haven, CT
29 October 2022

26074267R00059